Past Lives Eternal

Jenny Cockell

Copyright Jenny Cockell 2017

Introduction	3
Chapter 1- Who are we?	7
Chapter 2 -Finding Charles	24
Chapter 3 -The final journey	42
Chapter 4 -Going home	49
Chapter 5 -Time to let go	62
Chapter 6 -Between Lives-and other questions	70
Chapter 7 -Remember	83
Chapter 8 -Connectivity	97
Chapter 9 -What are we?	112
Chapter 10- Filling in the gaps	123
Chapter 11 -Carrousel	134
Conclusion	145

Introduction-

Reincarnation research provides us with cases and evidence about people who remember past lives, but leaves so many questions. Where do we go between lives? Does all life reincarnate? If our bodies are made of recycled star dust what about our souls; were they here too from the very beginning? There is a lot more beyond the essential validation provided by the accounts of children who remember past lives. It is probably time to move on and think more about the how and why.
So although this book started out as a means of sharing my final past life research, it became something more. I felt a need to try to address some of the many questions raised with answers and possibilities gleaned from research, experience and science.
When I started to write, several decades ago, my motivation at that time was partly to offer detailed evidence and unravel my own past life memories. In this book I do explore two more lives, including the successful conclusion of my short life in Gateshead during the Second World War. But over the course of writing I found that the questions offered me a much more challenging activity than a straightforward case study.
It was in 1993 that I published 'Yesterday's Children' ('Across Time and Death' in the USA) which chronicled my memories from childhood of a past life in Malahide, Ireland; I indicated where the village was and named it in childhood, indeed locating and finding the name of the village was the very first thing I did the first time I had my own atlas. My research continued through to tracing the family I recalled and being accepted by them.
This was followed by 'Past Lives Future Lives' which took a broader look at the subject and included experimental progression to possible future lives. It also looked at between lives and precognition, amongst other concepts. In 'Journeys Through Time' published in 2008 I uncovered some verification of memories of a life in Japan, also recalled from childhood.

However, the more interesting questions have always been about the nature of consciousness and how reincarnation might work in a practical sense. In the last chapter of this book I offer a fresh, alternate perspective on reality, referring to theoretical physics, which could explain reincarnation and quite a bit more.

Because I am often asked about aspects that might not otherwise occur to me, I have included a chapter with responses to the questions people ask most often, particularly about the between lives period. There are also sections where I try to consider fundamentals of our physical and psychological presence in the world. To ensure accuracy, references to scientific papers are included, though I try to keep the discussion here accessible and not too academic.

There are of course many ways to view any information, so sometimes I am asked how I respond to sceptics. I will answer that now. If someone using the same facts comes to a different conclusion, then that is an opinion and therefore has to be a valid reaction. Everybody sees the world slightly differently and draws conclusions from their own experience; it's not my place to tell other people how to think. With my past lives I just present the facts and chronicle the events as they happened, with as much detail and accuracy as possible. I hope I don't tell the reader what to think.

The only time I ever had a problem was when a prominent U.S. sceptic curiously decided to alter the facts, saying that I didn't name or locate the village of Malahide in childhood and had no idea where it was, despite the witness statements and subsequent independent research to the contrary. Gitti Coats researched and questioned witnesses for the BBC in 1990 and Mary Rose Barrington did the same for The Society for Psychical Research in 2002, also verifying with witnesses that I drew a map pinpointing the position of the house and named the village in Ireland as Malahide in childhood. Of course without the location I would never have started my search for the family or indeed been able to. In recent years I have found contact with people I haven't seen since school days and they sometimes mention the maps of Malahide I used to draw.

I find it difficult to understand why someone would alter the facts to fit a particular view point, as scientific method works from the facts towards a hypothesis. But I do understand that some people might be resistant to the idea of reincarnation so might unconsciously block out pertinent facts that they cannot accept, or fill in the gaps in their understanding without realising they are compromising the facts.

Mainly sceptics tend to dismiss all reincarnation cases as fantasy or imagination. This may seem harsh but there will always be a few claims to bolster this opinion. When someone says that they were a particular famous person and there are already five other people with the same claim, they cannot all be real. This is why verification is so important and why researchers have to be really thorough. It's also why the preference is to follow cases where the memory of past lives existed from childhood and of lives as ordinary people. This is so that information about the life could not have been gained from books, the Internet or other public sources.

In my own case the argument that the memory comes from imagination is more problematic. When I was diagnosed as being on the autistic spectrum, Asperger's syndrome, it was noted that I displayed very little creative or inventive imagination, made no creative comments or interpretations and was unable to make up a story.

The inability to make up an imaginative story is one of the many diagnostic features of Asperger's. I already knew that I had a very poor imagination, but even so was surprised at how bad it really was. I always dreaded creative writing at school because I had no idea of how to even begin a story. Although I referred in my first book to 'imaginary friends' in childhood, I was probably a bit too subtle. I was not referencing imagination as such but instead talking about seeing dead people; something that many children can do.

Like most autistics I prefer to deal with facts, detail and obsessive research. We can be innovative and creative in other ways, in science or art perhaps. But for many of us, telling an imaginative story, or even joining in with our own children's

Chapter 1

Who are we?

We all have an innate sense of who we are. We have a name, a place where we live, memory of our childhood and family members who have been with us along our journey through life. But we also have photographs, documents, phone numbers and probably a Facebook account. So we have memory which is backed up by evidence. We know who we are and can prove it.
But with a past life you begin with just the memory. Worse than that, probably because the memory has somehow been transferred from a previous body, some of the information is missing; there are gaps.
All reincarnation research relies completely on people's memories. So it's important that the recall is accurate. Young children are the best candidates. Many children remember past lives but those with excellent detail recall and good memories in general are more likely to be able to provide enough information to trace the person they once were; which is the objective. One of the reasons children are preferred is that we tend to forget our pasts, either partially or fully, as we grow up. When children get involved in school and with friends they tend to forget a lot of their earlier childhood years, which usually means that any past life memories are forgotten too.
Commonly a child remembering a past life will begin to talk about it at around the age of three, but generally stops by the age of six. It's normal for them to forget completely at this age.
The reason that most children who remember previous lives forget as they reach school age is probably because the brain wave patterns change as we grow up. Research has shown that babies and young children produce relaxing meditation type brain wave patterns (predominantly theta wave) that slowly change towards the more outward looking and aware adult patterns by school age. This can happen quite rapidly, as I

discovered when I was in contact with a family with a child who had past life recall a few years ago. A child can be talking vividly about a past life for several years, then within a few months it all stops.

It is possible that the brain wave changes occur in synchronicity with starting school. As many children now start school at four it is no surprise perhaps that children are commonly tending to forget past lives between the ages of four and five.

When a child suddenly starts talking about an event from the past it can be triggered by something in the present. For example a trip to the zoo might help a child to remember a different zoo trip in another life and another place. The child may come up with places or names; even if these seem unlikely make a note. I was once told about a surname that a child was using that seemed very odd. He said Hapt and his family queried the pronunciation, but the child had apparently insisted and upon further research the name appeared to originate from Austria. The same child told his family about death, which he likened to being sucked up into a tornado, then said that it was all right because soon you chose a new mummy and daddy and came back as a baby and decide to stay.

Yet less than a year later, having started school, this child's memories had faded so much that he thought they must have been a dream or made up. Soon they had gone completely. Resolution seems to have the same effect. Even many of the children whose previous life family have been traced by researchers or relatives and where contact is made and the case verified, they can completely forget.

If a child forgets their past life I would advise allowing it to remain forgotten. My observation is that most children have some past life memory, even if it is only small fragments. But we are probably meant to forget; I think life could be a whole lot easier without the extra memories. Though it could be that the sheer numbers of people alive today causes us to return too fast to be able to forget; in which case we might see an increase in the number of cases.

Some people suddenly recall a past life during adulthood, often after a trigger experience. They may just be remembering something that they had known in childhood but temporarily forgot, so it's not necessarily new information. These people might have presented with a past life memory in childhood that was not noticed or was ignored, so was forgotten about. Some researchers now take an interest in this adult group.

The detail of the past life memory can be used to track down the person recalled and with luck find the paperwork that confirms the life. For this reason accurate memory is essential.

Understandably, it is not an easy task. It takes a lot of time and concentration, even if the leg work is being done by the parents of a child who remembers or by a researcher. Doing it yourself as an adult may be easier, but as you read some of the accounts of self research you will find that most cases fail to conclude, which can be disappointing. However, there are many thousands of past life cases where the person has been identified; so it can be worth the effort. Though finding out all that you can is often enough to find peace, even if the person is not identified. And I feel strongly that what we seek is resolution and the ability to move on.

If a child starts to talk about a past life it is well worth making notes about what they say. In preference I wouldn't make a big deal about it in front of the child. You have to judge for yourself if the child is happy enough just to talk it through and then forget or if they need a more definite conclusion. In many cases the child will forget and be happier to concentrate on the here and now. I believe that the child's happiness is much more important than research. In many cases all the child wants is to be able to forget. However, making notes gives them an option if at a later stage they feel a need to follow it up.

I spoke about Mary and Malahide obsessively in childhood so my family and friends were in no doubt as to the location or detail. Several people who knew me in childhood also knew about some of my other memories, such as those of Japan. But I had no opportunity to trace the family I remembered until many years later. My parents didn't make notes but luckily I did, as well as drawing maps. Not forgetting the past as I grew up was a bonus, although I think I may have irritated a few people when as a teenager I obsessed about Malahide or Japan.

The only way to evidence a past life properly is to match details of the memory with facts about the person and at least some of these should not be publicly available. The best way to do this is to find someone who knew the person recalled. For this and other reasons it is very difficult, if not impossible, to confirm a case where there is no living relative or where the person was a public figure and details about their life are too readily available.

Although it is my Asperger's that is responsible for my difficulty with imagination, making my memory as a whole, more fact based, this is not typical for children who remember past lives. Researchers tell me that there are other autistic people who recall past lives, but it is not statistically relevant.

Clearly we need to be sure that the person remembering can tell the difference between real and imagined. But with children this is fairly easy, as they tend to describe past life events including things that they couldn't otherwise know about. Often they describe circumstances from an adult perspective and may talk about quite traumatic events in the kind of detail that a child wouldn't normally understand. So it should be fairly apparent when a child is talking about a past life rather than an imagined scenario. For example I came across a three year old who, on being given a toy sized suitcase, immediately started to play at being a door to door salesman carrying his wares, even though he had no experience of such a thing and neither had his parents. So past life research is driven by the memories we have that are unrelated to the here and now and often outside our normal experience. But what kind of detail do children, or adults, remember?

Firstly we have to look at the way usual memory works. What we recall from our life is events, with all of the detail but often out of context. So you might remember a school nativity play you were in at the age of five where you were one of the animals. You might remember wearing the costume; that it was imaginative games, is a non-starter. On the positive side we do tend to complete something we start and like to do 100% of the job, so are rather thorough.

This is probably why I needed to keep going until I was able to complete my research; to explore everything possible from the memories I had of other lives that had been with me since childhood. This is the last leg of the journey into my past lives and the questions and answers it prompted. In these memories I discovered the last pieces of the jigsaw that I hoped would finally set me free from the past.

itchy, that you didn't have to say any lines but were supposed to stand still. Maybe you will remember the smells of your school, of dust and chalk. You might remember some of your friends who were also in the play, but many people wouldn't be able to remember the names of all of the friends.

Past life memory is exactly the same; you recall events, how it felt, what was around you at the time, the people you were with. You probably won't remember many names but you are likely to remember things about some of the people. Maybe how they looked or if they were shy or kind or boisterous. Mostly you recall fragments, complete and detailed but isolated. So it might be like snapshots in time, including all of the senses, like how things looked or smelled or felt.

Just as you remember your current life as a whole variety of separate incidents, so you remember the past. Some of the memories might be prompted by dreams but mostly it tends to be very like normal memory and just thrown up apparently at random. Sometimes the events feel as though they are in the background and barely impinge on your life, at other time they become more prominent. In other words past life memory feels exactly the same as any other memory in that you might recall past events at any time.

What you won't be able to remember are things like your telephone number, national insurance number or precise dates, although the time scales with rough dates are often known. This could be because when we go through early childhood in this life, details such as numbers and exact dates are discarded as unimportant or irrelevant to the child. Or it may be something to do with the way memory is transferred between lives. Perhaps our soul doesn't consider numbers to be an important part of our identity. The things that are important to us and that we reflect upon are the personal events in our lives. Memory is often very subjective; past life memory is almost entirely about what we saw and how we felt.

When I first started researching past lives I was concerned that my memory wasn't perfect, I couldn't remember surnames properly, some of the smaller details were not completely right.

Even after writing the first book I found that I had indicated the wrong butcher's shop in Malahide; the right one was around the corner. But I included the mistakes when I wrote about my experiences because it seemed honest to do so and it was part of the process. I have always felt strongly about things being done correctly.

Many years later I discovered that serious academic researchers into reincarnation cases look at the little mistakes as an indication of real memory, because real memory is not perfect. It is the cases where people claim to recall every name and every detail completely accurately that are less likely to turn out to be real memory.

So perhaps the first thing to bear in mind is just that; memory is not perfect. If you have what appears to be past life memory, or you have a child who begins to talk about another time or place, write everything down but don't worry too much about the recall of exact names. There will probably be some precise details but it is usually of particular events from a personal perspective. There may be names but don't pressure for unrealistic accuracy. With a child just see what you get and don't push them. Wait patiently for them to talk some more and don't upset them. The child is much more important than the memory of their past.

What do I remember from past lives? Exactly what I have described; many isolated fragments in detail. I know where and when and who I was at the time, just as you know how old you were when remembering an event from your childhood. Although I always had a pretty good idea of when, for me location was always the strongest and most reliable point.

As a child I spoke about Mary in Ireland before the age of four and later, as a primary school child, identified Malahide as the location on my atlas, bought for me by my father. Although Malahide was just marked with a dot on the atlas, throughout childhood I drew maps of the village, pinpointing the exact position of the house, whilst sitting at the dining room table, with my mother and brothers looking on. None of the detail of my map was confirmed until decades later. I was able to match one of my childhood maps to a purchased map of the area, in the company of the bookshop owner who had ordered the map for me in the 1980s. The house position was eventually confirmed as correct by a local man in 1988.

I also remembered living in Japan and described almost as many events there. Once again, the location which I talked about in childhood was the key to tracing the family. I didn't use any hypnosis to augment the Japan memories.

There were many other fragments. Some of these were to do with my most recent life in Gateshead, some related to different lives much further back in the past.

It's possible that a number of factors helped my memories to remain. I have most of the autistic co-morbids; these are added complications that very often occur alongside autism spectrum disorder. So in childhood I struggled with a degree of attention deficit disorder, so was to some extent isolated with my own thought and memories. I had to cope with auditory processing problems, meaning that at times I had difficulty listening. I struggled for many years at school because I am dyslexic, have dyscalculia (number problems) and dysnomia (difficulty remembering words or in my case names). Also, because I didn't understand imagination I had difficulty playing games with other children so tended to sit out and spend time with my own thoughts. All of these aspects may, in my case, have an important relevance. Not to my having past life recall in the first place but perhaps to my continuing to remember.

When we remember past lives we are reflecting on a time when we were not quite the same person, we may not even be the same gender or race; we may have looked different. So what we are remembering is ourselves, but with different genetics, a different physical body and sometimes a very different upbringing. So it makes you wonder what part of us is reincarnated.

A few years ago I built up a family tree and eventually managed to track down and communicate directly with a number of half cousins, second cousins and a handful of third and fourth cousins. This was mainly because I like to research everything thoroughly and enjoyed contacting relatives. But it also gave me a chance to find out about inherited factors. And since I had always been interested in analysing which part of us continues, it gave me a chance to consider how much of our personality is purely inherited. So I asked every contact about a variety of inherited traits.

Most of the medical inheritance was easy to trace through the different branches of the family. But there were also other themes repeated. An interest in genetics that my mother and I share was reflected in a second cousin who was a geneticist. And a number of people along my grandmother's side were outstanding mathematicians, like my brother and one uncle. Some traits were easy to identify as genetic, like the height from my grandmother's side where many of the women were quite tall; curiously exactly the same height, 5 ft 10inches. But others seemed more personality based, like a fear of heights.

After many questions and much thought I came to the conclusion that a great deal of what we think of as our identity is driven by genetics; but that we are still individual. Perhaps the real self is the observer, the part of us that experiences everything from within the inherited body with its inherited brain function.

A child may remember being quite a different person to the present. Yet there still seem to be some personality constants that cannot relate to genetics. Although a few people appear to return to the same family, so are still related to that family in their return and therefore share genetics, most of the past lives are unrelated.

Although most cases concentrate on children who recall past lives, there are many adults on their own quests. Maybe a few like me always remembered and didn't forget as they grew up, but for many adults memories can emerge quite suddenly. The trigger can be a trip to a strangely familiar place or an unexpected experience, even an odd smell. Sometimes quite a small reminder can trigger past life memories to rise into the conscious mind. Because smell is linked directly with memory, this is not an unusual trigger. The reason smell has a direct link is believed to be because smelling and tasting food plants is linked with remembering the smell of those that turn out to be toxic; so it is a primal ability to do with survival and as a consequence is deeply imbedded.

Some people find that meditation is an aid to memory, or re-remembering a past life that was known about in childhood but then forgotten. Certainly I found that meditation helped me sharpen up quite a lot of detail over the years. I have found that just thinking about any past life enables more memories to be discovered. You just need to prise open the door a little for memories to begin to slip out. Once the door is open, it is, in my experience, impossible to shut them out again completely. The same can be said of any memory, if you think about it the detail returns. Doing this with normal recall could provide useful practice.

The use of hypnosis is more problematical, partly because it is so easy to suggest memories or pressure for answers where there are none, which can lead to a false reply and the use of misdirection or imagination to complete a picture. I used hypnosis for some of my past life memories, though not all, but it was just to sharpen existing memory; though having said that I did find that the experience was helpful, especially in providing the initial confidence. It also brought up a few very accurate snippets of information; though in general meditation is considered a better way.

Why do some people remember past lives in the first place? Researchers agree that one of the strongest reasons to remember is unfinished business from the past that intrudes into our current life. We remember a past life when there was some disturbing event that was unforgettable and which wouldn't let us move forwards; something incomplete and unresolved. An early or sudden death is also cited.

My feeling is that this assessment is right; it certainly matches my own experiences. This would mean that I remembered my life in 1920s Ireland because I died young and left the children behind in untenable circumstances. I remembered 1860s Japan because I died young and failed in my duty and the life in

Gateshead because that was suddenly cut very short. There is a similar reason for every life recalled. If we had a problem that was not resolved we are more likely to remember.

I have been asked how many lives I remember; it's at least a dozen. Memory itself can be curious. During my exam taking years, if I could commit a single word from a page or larger section of text to memory, in the exam I could then recall the whole page as though photographically, using the single word as a trigger. This way it was possible to re-read the information in my mind in a 'virtual' book. So memory can be photographic. But past life memory holds to a different set of values; those of experiences over data.

Remembering the past is a much more introspective and unconscious. Like a half forgotten memory from childhood it sometimes needs to be coaxed. Learnt information is more easily forgotten than experiences, which may another reason why it is the things we felt about the past that remain rather than more useful detail.

Is the memory definitely from a past life or is it some form of clairvoyance? For me, the experience of past life memory is exactly what it appears to be, evidence of reincarnation; I feel that I was the person who's life I recall. It's not a second-hand access to someone else's life; what I recall is a personal, linear memory that is much the same as any other memory. I remember the feel of things, the sounds and smells, I recall being those people. It makes little difference if I think about things that happened in a past life or earlier in my current life. Although I am aware of the change in identity and time, they are still my own memories, my own lives.

Reincarnation can be described as the continuation of the soul from one physical life, through an interim period following physical death and then on into another life, in perpetuity. The part of us that moves on might be called the soul, the core personality or perhaps the energy of life.

This viewpoint, that it is what it looks like, is reinforced by memories of the deaths and of the period between lives, which gives linear continuity to the memory. Many people recall their deaths and the period between lives. I too have death memories and of reaching a place of light with a multitude of other life energies in a kind of timeless bright vortex or alternate dimension. Some people also remember the time just before returning and talk of the choice of their new life.

But other people may have their own interpretations that they feel fit better with their own experiences. We all have to find our own way of looking at the world, so I wouldn't try to dissuade anyone from holding a different view to my own. I have always hoped for tolerance of my views, so must therefore extend the same tolerance to others and accept that people may want to look at the experience in other ways to understand this phenomenon.

This flexibility is especially important when it comes to the relatives of the people from the lives I recall. Some of my past life family members have looked at it as the spirit of the deceased working through me. Sometimes other people feel that the memories are downloaded from a collective unconscious. Some see it as a form of clairvoyance. Until it's possible to prove the mechanism there is no overriding answer that must be accepted. But I have to write from my own viewpoint, my own sense of being and my own experience of the memories as being personal and of my own previous lives.

However, when people ask me if I 'believe' in reincarnation I usually say it's not a belief, it's a memory. For me it has never been about belief. This is probably because as a child I when I first spoke about past lives I was told that it was a belief, which I took to mean that it wasn't a reality. I found this a little disparaging at the time; even though I was only three.

The second aspect to consider is the research. These days research can be relatively easy, as long as you have detailed enough memories then some checking will be possible. It's worth watching or reading accounts of people who have been through this process; we all approach things differently and there are often many ways to find what you are looking for. You might need to think creatively or laterally about how to start your search, especially if the details of the memory seem sparse.

But a word of warning, take care that your research is accurate, for two reasons. Firstly the research is the basis for evidence and should be as transparent as possible and secondly, you don't want to contact the wrong person, someone who has no connection to your previous life. It's hard enough for everyone when you get it right but to get it wrong would be very difficult.

If the memory includes an event, say a fire in a factory, you might be able to search online for factory fires. If a time span is included in the memory it could help reduce the search to a particular factory fire. This could then indicate a location. Cross referencing remaining memories into this location could narrow it down even further.

There is however a flaw with online research when it comes to tracing a name, unless it is related to an event that was reported. If you only have the first name of the person you remember then you cannot look at records of births online. This is because you need a surname in order to check births. If you can find a records office still storing micro-fiche records then with these it's possible to look at a specific year and only look for people with the first name you remember, although be prepared, it is very time consuming. Although you might look at all births in an area in a particular year, the online record sometimes refuses to display when the numbers are too huge.

I did discovered however, that online on the free BDM site you can search marriages using a first name only, as long as you limit it to an area and a time frame. I found this because I was told that I have a half sibling. When my father was terminally ill he told me something he had never said to anyone. Just after his birthday in May of 1946, when he was still of school age, he was seduced by a Land Army girl some years his senior. He could only remember the woman's first name, Barbara, but saw her once again when she was heavily pregnant. He was never allowed to see the child. My sibling was probably born early 1947 and Barbara was last seen in May's Lane in Barnet with someone she may have married. So I was searching under marriages in Barnet with just the first name Barbara.

To date I still haven't found my sibling, but if you know the area you are searching this is another way to gain information. It is a great deal of information and will run into hundreds of people, but can be used as a framework and a starting point.

But if and when your research leads you to people related to your past life this brings another problem. How do you approach the people who were your family in a previous life; what do you tell them?

The questions that we seem to consider in unusual circumstances like this are, should I make contact, will this upset them and will they reject me? The answer is that it may well be a problem. You have to decide how much you need to resolve the memories and how considerate you can manage to be towards the other people you are about to engage with.

My own view is that if you have spent a lot of time and effort to trace someone from your past life then you really have a strong need to continue. So you know how you feel. You have no idea how the other person feels until you give them a chance to make up their own mind. To make their mind up they need to know the facts. To know the facts you have to contact them. You cannot think for other people or know beforehand how they will respond to you; you have to let them decide for themselves. As long as there are enough verifiable facts it is worth considering.

Obviously it's always important to be polite and try to be kind and to break the whole idea very gently. I tend to communicate better by letter so spend time beforehand planning what to say before it gets to the stage when contact is made. To have the greatest chance of acceptance it is important to think about the person you wish to meet and have respect for their feelings.

My biggest difficulty is that I get impatient and obsessive. So, even after all of my attempts to produce a kind letter and all of my rehearsals, I ended up in a first contact with one of Mary Sutton's sons by telephone; not ideal situation because I have a real problem communicating by telephone. Despite all of my best intentions and even though I was careful about how much I said it didn't go well; but I did at least get contact details for the oldest son, Sonny.

This meant I had a second chance to get it right. So, even though I ended up on the telephone again, I took it more carefully, making absolutely certain that I didn't mention the words 'reincarnation' or 'past lives'. I most definitely did not say that I was his mother. To do so at that stage would have been extremely inconsiderate.

After the phone call I panicked a bit and over the next week or so somehow managed to find myself in contact with a researcher working for the BBC. This was easier; the researcher met Sonny without me, allowing him time to get used to the idea and answer acceptable questioning without direct contact or any mention of the difficult stuff. By the time we did meet it was still very nerve-wracking, but at least the groundwork had been done.

We met in September 1990 and reminisced about Sonny's childhood in 1920s Ireland, comparing our memories and noticing how well our recollections of events and places matched. I still didn't mention reincarnation until we had seen each other a few times; I really didn't want to scare him off. By the time we talked about past lives he had worked it out for himself, so the transition was surprisingly easy. He accepted me.

With the next past life I researched it was even harder. I was invited to Japan by a television company but the whole thing was poorly thought out and marred by my overstressed reaction. The crew interviewed the very person I needed to meet, a member of the family I remembered, without me. I was left sitting in a vehicle with the interpreter and told to wait. The crew had no idea that they were interviewing a member of the family I recalled. The questions they asked were not remotely relevant and the opportunity to get things right was almost completely lost. Except that I am extremely persistent.

I learnt how to write in Japanese using a Japanese dictionary and a very strong magnifying glass to see the tiny lettering, so that I could copy each stroke of the characters. By using sentences written in the appendix section and substituting the verbs and nouns for ones I wanted, I produced sentences with the correct grammatical construction. Then I started to make my own enquiries.

But eventually it was help from Hisayo, a Japanese lady who helped me trace the right family, which is when she discovered that they had already been interviewed by the television company. Hisayo talked with the family member about the location of the home I remembered, which turned out to be a key memory. The house had been demolished long ago but my description and especially the precarious and exact position on the cliff edge provided the verifiable evidence and meant that I was accepted there too.

When you manage to be reunited with a past life family it is in some ways the beginning of a journey rather than the end. It isn't easy; it means that everyone involved has to face the complex array of emotions experienced in this unusual situation. Indeed I know of a number of people who have chosen not to tell their past life family about their memories for fear of rejection or ridicule, or just because the anticipated stress of the experience was too much of a concern. At some point you have to decide what is best to do.

I expect that the reason I always go ahead is due to some of my inherited Asperger's characteristics, like obsession and a driving need to find the right answers. I have to complete something once started and complete it as thoroughly as I possibly can. The way I do things will not be right for everyone.

In any past life research the members of the past life family themselves also have to cope with a difficult situation. They meet someone who claims to be a relative, apparently back from the dead, living again, usually as a young child, yet still able to remember their previous family and life. Or they have to find another explanation that they find more acceptable.

I think when faced with compelling evidence, when it is personal, it's hard for people to just shrug their shoulders and ignore it. But it is worth thinking about how you would cope if someone you loved came back in this way, tracking you down, finding you and talking about the past as though they had just been away on a long holiday. Yet looking different, sounding different and maybe not even being the same gender.

One thing people don't usually tell you is that when you meet your past life family you suddenly become aware of how different you are. You are talking with people you knew when you were in a different body a very long time ago. You know how much you have changed and how much time has passed and that you cannot quite be the person you were before, ever again. And you know that even though you have just found the people who you have been thinking about and wanting to be reunited with since you were a small child, everything is different now.

I have become very aware that time only goes in one direction. It's only at the moment you find the past family and sit face to face that you are hit with the realisation that you have to accept being who you are now. Curiously your memory; that has been held as though timeless, becomes a thing of the past as time catches up and the reality of the present seems to slap you in the face.

When you see a documentary about a child who remembers a past life, then that child is taken to visit the place they remember, you will see a sudden uneasiness and sadness in their manner. That is the moment that the reality of the present clashes with the memory of the past and the child realises that they can't go back.

This feeling is transient and passes. But it's part of a process of resolution that, at least in my own experience, has luckily been beneficial in the long term, but at the time it can be quite a shock. Life is all about moving forwards. Yet it is possible to have the best of both worlds, past and present together in our shifting perceptions. It just takes a bit of adjustment for everyone involved. If you are self researching though, it is something you need to be prepared for.

To be able to remain in contact with your past life family for many years is a definite bonus. Time allows the contact to evolve and there is a kind of catching up, where you feel able to be the self you are now. Still able to acknowledge who you were, but allow the past to be the past. Conversations move forwards and the past is mentioned less as the relationship evolves into a more normal friendship.

However, I always had another problem. Each time I was able to resolve one past life everything would readjust and for a while I was able to live in the present and enjoy life; but never for very long. Another past life always seemed to catch up with me. Memories I had talked about since childhood would edge more into focus. Vivid images and peculiar senses would creep back into my everyday world.

Chapter 2

Finding Charles

The memories of past lives are variable. Very often they are of vivid events but the images may seem isolated and be difficult to tie together.
This was not the case with my memories of my life as Mary Sutton which were always clear and in sequence. I always knew where the village was and the exact location of the house. I could remember the children and lots of events and details. Hypnosis did help bring these memories back in focus when I was an adult, mainly because the memories were already there anyway. But hypnosis, whilst reminding us of things slightly forgotten sometimes introduces error, so in the end I had to fall back on the original memory to find the family in Ireland.
However, I discovered that I knew far more than I thought, because every time someone asked me a question everything would just flood back. And the tiny details I gave in reply were found to be completely correct. This was especially useful when researchers asked me about things that I hadn't necessarily been concerned with before, like pets or building structure. It is exactly the same as remembering your childhood, the more you think about it the more you remember.
With my memory of Japan I didn't use any hypnosis to trace the family or to help with the memory, so had to concentrate more. But this memory too had been present since childhood so again, a little concentration helped. And again location was the most useful detail; I had always known the precise location of the house and where in Japan it stood, which was exceedingly helpful.
But for some past life memories, although the details may be very clear, tying them together and relating each fragment to one another might be harder. I remembered a life during the war years from earliest childhood, but until the hypnosis sessions and the eventual search for the family, I hadn't realised that

quite a few memory fragments from my childhood past life recollections actually related to this one life.

Some of the memories were so disturbing that I didn't want to think of them as being from any past life so tried very hard to forget. This might be why it took a back seat for so long. But for this particular life I do have to thank hypnosis for jogging my memory. It brought back what I already knew in childhood, but at last let me make sense of it all. It was also some vindication for hypnosis as a past life recall tool.

Hypnosis did introduce a few errors however, as is often the case. When asked to see my death as Charles, I went instead to a time when he was ill, mumps I think, a few months before the death. But it did remind me of the layout of the room downstairs where I was being looked after and of the lady who was looking after me.

When I at last started to search seriously for this particular life, as a boy in the years of the Second World War, I had for the previous year or so been responding to some rather insistent mental prompting to research another life as a boy in the 1600s. I discuss this research later in the book, but at the time its importance was probably to get me to think more about being a boy so that I would get on and research the more recent life that I had been ignoring for so long.

People sometime wonder if there is a problem swapping around between genders from life to life, but there really isn't. The difference between male and female is not as great as might be imagined. The physicality is different but there is a huge overlap in personality. Most people have a mixture of traits that are considered masculine or feminine. Commonly people have about 60% characteristics of their own gender and 40% of the other, but this is very variable. There are plenty of tests to try this out which may surprise you.

In other words, gender changes between lives need not be a huge problem. The other side of it, the physical aspects, are probably taken care of with hormonal and physiological controls. Though there are reports of some people having problems which I discuss in a later chapter.

The memory would sneak up on me at odd moments; I would just stop and glance down at my legs with a sudden thought that the lower legs had gone completely. This would occur whilst I was walking up stairs a number times and in the back of my mind was the thought that I shouldn't be able to walk at all, because I only had part of my legs left. I mentioned it to my family from time to time, but since we all knew that it was just another past life memory and wasn't anything physical nothing was done.

Many times I would wake up with the sensation of lines drawn just below the knees and on the ankles, as though a section of the legs had been marked somehow at the edges of the crushed area. The marks were at a slight angle across the lower legs, higher on the right. At other times it was more graphic. Below the crushed legs my feet had no feeling; they seemed isolated, without nerves. I am sure I tried to sit up during the accident as a matter of reflex, to look at the legs and feet. It's no surprise that I spent so much of my life trying to ignore it or think about other things to do.

It was many years before I even began to follow up my life as Charles. The memory had been stimulated by seeing it again under hypnosis in the 1980s which is when I gave the name and may have been the time that I started to realise that the fragments I had always recalled were of the same life.

What I described under hypnosis was the time period, which was during the years of the Second World War, specifically 1939 or 40 to 1945. And I gave a first name, then struggled a bit with a surname but seemed to recall the starting letter. So I said Charles S with some certainty and clarity, suggesting that I had always known this name. This gave me a useful starting point. Also triggered by hypnosis I saw a road name with a double L and an e in it.

The lucky thing was that I also had a fairly detailed memory of the house and surrounding area, particularly the journey down the road to school. The house was also present in quite a bit of detail from childhood and ongoing dreams and memory that I hadn't realised went with this particular life. I often spoke to people about my house and said I was still looking for it, without having completely associated it with the Charles memory. I remember my husband's accountant asking me in the 1980s if I had found my house yet. I said I hadn't.

But for the first time with any of my past life memories I had no strong sense of a geographical location, possibly due to the age of the child. All of the location memories were limited to a small area walked around and well known. This was a problem; I needed to find the town.

I remember being walked to school down the road and I was the only child with my mother, holding her left hand with my right, which placed me on the inner side of the pavement as we walked down on the left side of the road. It stuck in my mind because I was allowed to walk slowly, at my own pace; I wasn't hurried and my mother wasn't stressed at all but gentle and patient. My hand was held most of the time but gently.

This was in contrast with my current life childhood where my mother used to walk quite fast, taking me along by my hand so that I had to walk very quickly or jog to keep up, probably because I was easily distracted and took too much time. The firm grip, in hindsight, may have been because I constantly fidgeted my hands even when they were held, which I know was annoying, but I couldn't help it. I would click out my hyper-flexive thumbs as a constant stimming, which must have been irritating.

After having seen the memory under hypnosis it helped me to realise that I had always remembered the journey to school, the house and a number of other details; they all came from this same life. So in this case hypnosis helped me to bring together what had previously been some very detailed but somewhat disjointed memories, into a cohesive whole.

Because I had previously conducted my past life searches using location first, I initially I tried to use the same method as I had with my Irish memory. But this time I was seeing everything from the viewpoint of a small child, which was not very helpful. I tried to use visual pointers to determine location but was led astray and began looking in quite the wrong area. I was relying on something seen under hypnosis because I thought there was no other starting point.

With hypnosis I had seen initials on the road sign that I thought were NE. To me as an adult that meant North East London. So I spent ages driving down and looking for streets in North East London and not recognising anything. I had also recalled the name Raymond under hypnosis and assumed it was the father's name because that was the question I had been asked about.

But after a while I had to accept that I was looking at it wrongly, so I would be better to try looking at it another way. Because I had a good clear image of the first name and initial from hypnosis and had always had an indication of the dates, it made more sense to use those details as the starting point. The era, the Second World War period, was something that I had always associated with the truck fears, which helped.

When I eventually got around to a proper search for Charles I went with my mother, who volunteered to assist, to the records office in Hertford. We had an allocated time slot and my mother had booked us in for several hours each visit. I decided that we should look at deaths in the post war period with several years either side to allow for error. We were looking for the death of all children named Charles at the age of six, but also looking at any between the ages of four to eight, just to be on the safe side.

We were working in tandem on different sections to cover the years we needed to check and list any finds as we went. We worked steadily and as efficiently as we could, carefully studying many micro-fiche records under the specially set up microscope viewing machines. We had to get through the entire records for the period; there were no Internet records then, so it was a very time consuming process. This meant looking at all of the death records for the whole country over a four year period, because I was aware that the dates I recalled were generally right but not necessarily spot on.

Although this seems to be a very laborious process compared with using the Internet I believe we were lucky to be able to use the micro-fiche records. Everything is now on computer and in some areas there is no way to access either micro-fiche or paper records. Other researchers have complained to me that they cannot use the new records systems for a past life search because it is now impossible to search without a surname, because the search engine requires a surname.

This is a particular problem in Scotland where all records are on computer only. This might also be a problem for people researching to compile statistical data where they need to pick out certain details from all of the records. So we were fortunate to be searching at the time we did and were able to look for Charles's records before everything was consigned to Internet sites.

We listed every name of every child who died at about the right age and in the right time slot. I still have the notes we made. And we were extremely lucky; there was only one Charles in the whole country with a death at the right age and at the right time. Helpfully this Charles also had a surname beginning with S. It turned out that I had the year and age right too. This was such a relief because it had made the search a lot easier; there was only one possibility, only one choice. If I had got the details right then we had found Charles. All I had to do now was see if the other details matched.

This Charles, Charles Savage, was born in Gateshead. However, the birth certificate which was issued to me in December 1994, gave an address in Askew Road. When I checked the location against a street atlas I could see straight away that the road layout was completely wrong, the streets were nothing like the drawings I had made and there was no school where I expected to find one. This disappointment caused me to abandon the search for several years, because I assumed that I was wrong. I didn't think that there was much chance that I would ever be able to resolve this case.

Then one day I was thinking about it and it occurred to me that just because Charles was born at this address didn't mean that this was where he grew up, so I tried again. It was almost eight years later in August 2002 when I finally sent off for the death certificate. When it came, sure enough, at the time of death, at the age of six in 1945, Charles was living at a different address

Since early childhood I had frequently woken with the memory of my lower legs being crushed, but fortunately without any memory of pain. While I was researching the life from the 1600s this particular memory had become increasingly persistent until it was happening virtually every day. I had researched enough by this point in time to know that it was a memory of the injuries that took the life of Charles Savage in Gateshead in 1945. I began to realise that I had been coping with this on and off for nearly 59 years, but had been trying to push it aside. I wanted to ignore it because the accident was unpleasant and the sense of loss hard to cope with. But eventually I knew time to do something about it.

My childhood recollections of this war time life had been fragmented and I managed to shut most of it away. It had not been as persistent as the memories of the life as Mary Sutton or even of the Japanese Hanafusa girl, so had been largely ignored despite the frequent waking experience recalling the injuries. But perhaps because I had resolved the other lives the memories had become increasingly to the fore in later years.

As a five or six year old child I had been troubled by dreams of being pursued by a small truck that seemed determined to run me over, even mounting the pavement to get me. These dreams bothered me so much that when I walked to school I was always nervously on the look out for vehicles that might mount the pavement. When I was a little older and allowed to cross roads by myself I used to take a long time waiting for the road to be completely empty before crossing. I was an overcautious road crosser; this is probably still the case.

Although the dreams stopped once I passed the age of six, I still woke from time to time for the rest of my life with the memory of crush injuries; or sometimes it would happen at odd moments during the day. But after all of the more pressing memories had been resolved this was disturbing me on a virtually daily basis and was a prominent and distressing experience. Neither the injuries nor the truck mounting the pavement were ever explored under hypnosis so I relied only on the childhood recall for these important details.

in Elliott Road, Gateshead. Also the cause of death given on the death certificate was described as 'injury accidentally sustained as a result of being run over by a motor lorry'. A chill went down my spine. I suddenly realised that I had the right person after all; the cause of death was an absolute clincher for me as it tied in perfectly with my memories of the crush injuries and made sense of the memory.

[Certified Copy of an Entry of Death, HC 849929, Registration District Gateshead, 1945, Death in the Sub-district of Gateshead Second, in the County Borough of Gateshead. Entry for Charles Hardwicke Savage, Male, 6 years, Son of Charles Edward Savage deceased a General Labourer of Elliott Road. Cause of death: Injuries accidentally sustained as a result of being run over by a motor lorry. No P.M. Certificate received from William Carr Coroner for the West Chester Ward of Durham. Inquest held on the 22nd October 1945 and by adjournment on the 26th Nov 1945. Nineteenth October 1945, Elliott Road, Gateshead. When registered: Twenty Sixth November 1945. 13 Aug 02.]

This death certificate was therefore instantly a very useful piece of information. Elliott Road matched the 'e' and double L road name that I had described after I remembered running my finger over the street sign tracing the letters whilst under hypnosis. The omission of the door number on the certificate was sorted out with a quick phone call to the records office where the clerk apologised, gave me the number and said he forgot to write it on.

When I managed to find a rather old copy of a Gateshead and Newcastle Street Atlas the road layout looked completely right. At last I began to feel more confident and hoped that I could be on the right trail. I was no longer being held back. But that also meant that I would have to go forwards. I would have to go through that stressful experience of immersing myself in the past, with all the inner turmoil it creates. And I knew it also meant coping with an obsessive need that I wouldn't be able to quell until the task had been completed. It's a bit like finding you are pregnant with a second or third child; you remember what you will have to go through in order to get to the good bit and there is no way of avoiding the pain.

I started to talk about the research and knew that at some point I would need to visit Gateshead, but it was a long journey to make with only a little to go on and I always panic about journeys. However, a reader and his wife, Brian and Evelyn Thomas, kindly offered to visit the house whilst they were on holiday in the area in August 2005, some three years after I first acquired the death certificate. This would be a helpful scouting party.

When Brian returned he said that the house layout was completely correct and just as I had described it; a double fronted house with a path at the left; the house from my dreams that I had been looking for. The road layout was also right, although the road had been altered, cut across with a green area as part of a traffic calming scheme. Also the school at first appeared to be in the wrong place.

Brian said he couldn't find the school and he marked the new school on a sketch map he made; it was in the wrong place. But this didn't worry me, the old street map I had showed that the original war time school was on the road I had indicated on my sketch of the area, exactly where I expected to find it.

After this confirmation I wrote to the occupiers of the house asking if they knew anything about the current whereabouts of the previous family. The lady of the house wrote back telling me that she was fairly new to the area but told me about a neighbour who had lived in the road for at least 50 years.

It's possible that if I had followed up and got in touch with the neighbour I could have completed the search at that stage. But I was still holding back and foolishly the opportunity was never taken. I was too nervous to move forwards. This might seem absurd but I get overwhelmed with too much happening or too much change. This was going to be a lot to cope with and I needed time to prepare; I was shutting down to reduce the overload. It was a bit more than I could do just then.

All of this research had taken a very long time. Initially I hadn't even pieced the memory together enough to start a search and it had very much taken a back seat to the more pressing concerns for Mary Sutton's children. Then it was pushed aside again while I felt a need to find out more about living in Japan prior to living in Ireland as Mary.

There was another reason it had taken a long time to get started on this research. It had been surprisingly difficult to adjust to life once I had traced the Sutton family. None of the work on past lives that I had read about or seen looked at it from the perspective of the person remembering. I had not been prepared for the sense of dislocation.

I had to accept that my old family were not only grown up but they were all over retirement age; so my time with them was going to be limited. And I also had to take on board that even though I remembered my life as Mary I was not Mary now, I was different and a lot of time had passed.

Going public with the story was also double edged. I needed to share the story; it was one of the few ways to cope with the strangeness of the experience, by externalising. And sharing was the right thing to do to help others. This was important to me because I had wanted that help as a child but it was nowhere to be found. I felt that the least I could do was help normalise the subject matter so that others might be better placed to find help and to understand the process. Being able to discuss the events and the whole concept of reincarnation to an interested audience was a relief, cathartic in itself and enjoyable.

Yet I am an extreme introvert and dislike attention, so talking on interviews and giving lectures was demanding and draining, so required a lot of down time to recover. Consequently I had lost many years when I could have been researching and finding Charles's family; I wasn't sure if I was ready to go through it again. I needed time to let everything settle.

Because the whole process of finding past lives had already been overwhelming I allowed myself to be distracted with other avenues of research, travelling to lectures and with publicity. On top of that there were changes and challenges in my current life. So sadly I didn't really concentrate on my life as Charles until time took my older family, my Sutton children, away from me again. This time though, it had been a bit easier to let go; we had many years together to resolve our concerns over the past.

When I started to look further, to try to find out more about the Charles's mother, I couldn't find a second marriage, so was unable to begin to search for her. In any case I was very nervous about trying to trace her because she had lost her child and if I turned up talking about it I would only be reminding her of this loss. My presence in her life could make it worse rather than better. I didn't think it was fair to take that risk. I have always been concerned not to cause upset, so I think I neglected the search even longer, because it worried me so much.

I often wondered if the mother was still alive; time passed but I still needed to know, even if I didn't have the courage to meet her. I checked the records and found her birth entry for the March quarter of 1919, but as years went by I realised that the chance of her still being alive was becoming more and more remote. I wondered if I could find her, maybe meet her, but not tell her why. But that seemed wrong somehow, not honest.

However, I wanted to find out more, though try as I might I could not trace her or even find a death certificate for her. Perhaps she had remarried, but searching for details of any marriage at the records office, which was still open for business at the town library, proved fruitless. I wasn't doing very well.

In my later searches I wondered if reading a copy of the inquest would help. I had discovered that the inquest was held on 22 October 1945 and by adjournment 26th November 1945. This was written on the death certificate under the section marked signature, description and residence of informant.

To find out more I got in touch with the Durham County records office in 2011 and requested a copy of the inquest, if it was still available, giving the details quoted on the death certificate. The very kind archivist at the records office was unable to find the inquest and told me that many of the older files had been destroyed. She even went to the trouble of checking one of the newspapers from the time to see if it had been mentioned, but it was not.

Charles died on the 19th of October 1945; the Second World War ended on 2nd September and the United Nations was formed on 24th of October. I think the newspapers probably had more pressing things to talk about. The archivist had suggested visiting the Durham newspaper archives to see if I might have any better luck than her, but it felt like a long journey to go on chasing something that might not be found. I wasn't quite ready to visit the area yet and was somewhat aware that I was still reticent.

Then, out of the blue in August 2012, one of my readers, Teresa Gregory McMillan, contacted me; she had found more information about Charles Savage. I had already found a possible birth date for his mother Margaret, and knew that his father Charles Edward Savage had died during the war years and presumably as a soldier. What I hadn't found was the younger brother born in 1940, which Teresa had, or any second marriage for Margaret.

But I hadn't been looking hard enough or thinking hard enough. I had seen other boys in my memories but not even thought about one of them being a brother. This was a serious failure. Now she mentioned it this seemed so right and I was overjoyed at the thought of finding a brother, a living relative. It was very exciting; I kept thinking about it, a brother, my brother.

If this was the right marriage it appeared to be very close to the date when Charles died; a period I had not thought to look at, but one that should have been obvious. Many soldiers were away for the entire war, the whole six years, but in 1945 all of the men returned. Quite suddenly there would have been a lot of men about, some of whom would want to forget the war and move forwards with a normal life. Perhaps this man was someone Margaret had met when he was on leave and they married as soon as he was discharged.

Teresa found not only the marriage details for December 1945 but there were also more children in this second marriage; there were two half siblings, a sister born in 1946 and a brother in 1948. Quite quickly we had a number of people who might be part of this family, my previous family. It was beginning to get very exciting.

We sent off for the marriage certificates and birth certificates to check the details and make sure that we had the right people; the details given on the records online were not enough to be certain, so certificates were the only way to be sure. So I logged on to the certificate ordering site and ordered certificates.

I now wanted to search any and every possible avenue. So, whilst waiting for the brother's birth certificate, which I had sent for, and the marriage certificate, which Teresa had sent for, I contacted someone on Facebook who Teresa thought could be the brother; he kindly replied but it turned out that he wasn't. I also contacted several people on Friends Reunited in the off chance of finding the half sister. The useful thing about Friends Reunited was that women were listed under both their maiden names and married names. So if someone was listed, it saved having to try to find marriage certificates, which can be problematic when there are many possibilities. But this didn't help either.

Because there was now a chance that I might manage to trace a family member I had to think very carefully about how to approach any contact that could be confirmed as a relative of Charles. I had been at this place before with the Sutton family. I wanted contact but didn't want to spook anyone. But even having been through it before was not going to make the task easier, because the family I wanted to get in touch with had not been through it before. You would think that at least it would be easier for me, but it never is. First contact with someone from a past life is exciting and at the same time daunting; a curious mixture of joy and fear.

I needed resolution but always had to be very aware of people's feelings. This was the trickiest part of the whole process and I found it immensely stressful; which is probably part of the reason I had been putting the whole thing off for so long. There was no way it could be easy because it involved other people and needed diplomacy. So even though it was an exciting and compulsive roller coaster that I couldn't slow down even if I wanted to, I began to loose sleep worrying about it and was aware that I was panicking all the time. My anxiety levels were sky high.

Within the next few weeks Teresa amazingly managed to produce a partially complete family tree, which we both added to as more information came in. She also found a relative of Charles's on Facebook. Teresa then found someone related to Charles's aunt, who had produced a detailed family tree on an online site. This gave us a lot more information about Charles's father, who had died in 1942 in Egypt at the age of 26 and had been awarded a number of medals. Charles's grandfather had come from Armagh in Northern Ireland.

More importantly we discovered that Charles's mother Margaret had died in 1999. I was saddened by this, I had wanted to be able to meet her, in a dichotomous way, and had I been a bit quicker this would have been possible; but it did mean that I no longer had to worry about upsetting her. This meant that I felt a little better able to go ahead and complete the research; it was one fewer thing to worry about regarding contact with the family.

Oddly, if Teresa hadn't stepped in when she did I'm not sure how much longer I might have procrastinated, despite the constant reminder of the accident most mornings. But now, with a bit of a nudge and my enthusiasm growing rapidly, the real search was on. We now had enough information to track down Charles's brother.

I got in touch with both of the people Teresa had found on Facebook, saying that I was looking for relatives of Charles's mother, Margaret, and waited to see if either would reply. I wasn't sure what I would do if there was no reply. And if there was a reply how could I explain how important this was to me without scaring people off? Particularly as it was not an easy thing to say in a few words on a Facebook message box.

The only response I had at this stage was via e-mail from the lady Teresa had contacted through the online genealogy site. This lady turned out to be married to the son of one of Charles's first cousins. She was able to fill in many of the important details, including about Charles's brother's marriage and his family. So I was able to confirm that Teresa had found the right marriage details even before the certificate of marriage arrived.

Using the online phone book I managed to find a few possible addresses and wrote to the people at these addresses, and I had some kind replies, but none matched. Eventually, to find the right address I found and used a free offer for a one off search on a people finding site, and then played a game of logic with a census site that only gives limited information without payment. I used an elimination process. By swapping out the brother's name with his wife's name and the different addresses I had, I was able to reduce the number of choices to one partial address, without having to pay a fee.

I realised that I was just playing games of logic as a means of rather irresistible distraction and procrastination, so decided to get on with it and pay the fee. So I found the brother's full address and also in the end I found his half sister's address too. I seemed to think that I needed as many family addresses as possible to hedge my bets, I didn't know if anyone would want to reply to me. I was over thinking the whole process, as I usually do.

It was time to be brave and make contact. I was very nervous.

This was September 11th 2012. I wrote to Charles's brother, who was now 72. I enclosed a copy of the family tree which I hoped was mostly right, a stamped addressed envelope and a request to reply if he was the person I had been searching for. I promised to explain my connection to the family.

Because I was able to locate several more family addresses I also wrote to Charles's half sister. I had decided that I should write to everyone I had an address for, or e-mail, on the same day and tell them all what this was about. This was partly because I expected rejection and partly because I tend to try much harder than is needed.

I kept getting up very early in the morning, in the dark and often at 3.00am, to compose letters that I could send along with a copy of my latest book and a copy of the film. This, I thought, might be the best way to explain what was going on. But I still expected rejection.

I have often found the early hours are good for working through difficult thoughts or ideas but I was becoming quite tired and stressed; though very focussed. This was the most difficult, crucial stage. I kept reminding myself that it was important to try to get it right and to say the right things.

In the end I was so sure that nobody would reply that I decided to send the explanations before anyone had time to answer the initial enquiries, to save myself disappointment. I fine tuned the letter I wanted to send and just changed the first few lines to suit each recipient.

For politeness sake I made sure that they knew that the letters were almost identical. For the brother I also enclosed a copy of the film of 'Yesterday's Children' and my most recent book 'Journeys Through Time' because it had a brief section about Charles at the back. The half sister also got a book; I had bought plenty of copies for friends and had a number left over, but I hadn't thought about buying more copies of the film in time so had sent Charles's brother my own copy.

The letter started with an apology for writing again without waiting for a reply and an admission that I was nervous and found this difficult to explain. It went on-

There are three families I have spent my whole life trying to trace. I found the first more than 20 years ago. This relates to memories of 1920s Ireland and I was very lucky, because a BBC researcher helped me at the point of first contact and put together a long list of the details that I remembered about the family, most of which were things that only they knew- and they completely accepted me, for which I was very grateful. This family, the Sutton's, decided that they wanted to go public with the story and I ended up writing a book. We all did documentaries and there was even a film. To this day the family is still happy that it went public- to my relief.

The second family was to do with the time of the Meji restoration in 1860s Japan. I managed to locate descendants in 2007. After providing them with information, including specific details about a house now long gone, this family also accepted me, but were much more private. They were happy for me to write about events from the past but asked me to keep the modern day family names private- which of course I honoured completely.

Now at last I have found my third family, the Savage family, and I am very concerned because however many times I go through this process it doesn't change, it is difficult. I don't expect people to accept me but hope for the chance to explain. Obviously I can keep things private this time if that is what the family want.

Because of previous publicity you can find out a lot about me by going online to 'you tube' and type in my name. The 'Strange But True' documentary is useful because you can see my Irish family, the Sutton's, and they say what they think about it.

I come from a scientific background and always need a great deal of evidence, so expect you to need evidence too. I hope I can provide enough for you.

This is what I remember and why I needed to find you. All my life I have had memories of lives from the past. One of these memories is relevant to your family- I have since childhood woken up from time to time with the image of crush injuries to my legs (but no memory of pain). For the last year this has happened every morning, so I knew I would have to resolve it now. As a five or six year old I had nightmares of being chased and run down by a lorry outside my house; I now know these memories are connected.

Because I had other memories that were more detailed, this memory got neglected, and as I grew up a lot of the detail became less prominent. I used hypnosis to help in the 1980s, and although I don't really trust hypnosis it did help me remember details that were later confirmed as accurate.

I can remember the life of a boy who lived between 1939- 45 and was specific about those exact years. I could remember the name Charles but had only S for the surname. I could describe a house and street in some detail. The road name had a double L in it. When I checked records in the 1990's there was only one person in the whole country who fitted the description. He was Charles Hardwick Savage. When I found he lived in a road with a double L just as I remembered I was encouraged. In 2005 I wrote to the current owner and she confirmed my description. Friends also visited the area later that year and were also able to confirm that my description of the house and street were accurate. I have never been to Gateshead myself.

I remembered walking down the street to school, crossing the road and going right, the school was on the left of that road not far along. I checked a map and couldn't find the school, then got an older map and found St Winifred's junior and infants school on Marigold Avenue exactly in the right place. I have since found that the old school was demolished, but I still remembered where it was.

I can remember playing alone a lot, and two games, one was playing with the cobwebs in the bushes near the back door, the other was playing on the curb with one foot in the gutter so that when you walk you go up and down with each step. I had one childhood illness because I remember being ill and lying in the front room, the one to the left of the front door.

I went on to say briefly that I would be grateful for any response and would love to be able to drive up to Gateshead and meet anyone from the family who would be willing to talk to me. I acknowledged that they might not be comfortable with the concept. And because it is such a strange thing I always expect rejection, but must still try.

I didn't really expect a reply.

Chapter 3

The Final Journey

On Monday September 17th 2012 I found that a phone call with a Gateshead prefix had been made to my phone. There was a message on the answer-phone too but I didn't even notice that. I phoned back immediately, I was too nervous to spend any time thinking about it or what I might say. It was John Savage, Charles's younger brother. John said that he was quite happy for me to 'write it up'. We had a long chat about Charles and the old home. He told me more about the accident.

Some of the local boys would sit on the back of the milk float as it went door to door. Charles was sitting on the float with a few other boys and they all got off. Charles jumped down, but he caught his foot as he jumped and then he fell on the footpath just as the vehicle was reversing into a neighbours' drive. The driver thought that the boys had all got off and didn't notice Charles on the ground right behind his vehicle. Charles went right underneath as it reversed over him. As John spoke I was visualising the accident in slow motion and reliving it.

My own recall of the accident was that there was some impact to the right side of the body; in retrospect this could have been the fall from the lorry. I felt slightly winded and was lying with my feet at the driver's side of the vehicle and my body across the back. Then the lower legs were then completely crushed from knee to ankle, presumably by going under a wheel. The crush injury to the lower legs was slightly at an angle in that the injury to the left leg was slightly lower down, by no more than a couple of inches. Presumably this was the angle at which the wheel rolled across the legs. The width of a tyre relates well to the length of a six year old child's lower leg, knee to ankle, this would explain the crush memory perfectly. I don't remember anything at all beyond this point.

There was going to be no way of confirming the detail of this, unless someone had kept a copy of the inquest that I wasn't able to find, so I didn't discuss it further at this point. To do so seemed unnecessarily harsh. I didn't want to talk about it on the phone anyway, the telephone is too impersonal and I didn't want to upset John by going over the accident in gory detail. But it was interesting that the accident happened on the pavement, because it made sense of my childhood dream of being chased onto the pavement by a small truck.

For further detail I looked into the history of milk delivery. Just after the war, milk was often still delivered by horse and cart. Several of my elderly patients remembered this when I asked them over the next few days. Even in cities horses were often used. My mother, who was born in 1930 also remembers the era well and said the same thing. But in some places the horse and cart had been replaced with a small lorry, especially in cities where horse excrement was considered more of a problem on the roads. This lorry was similar to today's milk floats, but in 1945 might not have been electric. In 1941 Morrison Electrics standardised three body types for the quiet electric milk floats but they didn't go into production until after the war. So this van could have been a brand new quiet milk electric milk float, but more likely was just small diesel lorry. I expected it was the latter as this would tally with my recollections of a small lorry mounting the pavement and seemed to fit the description John was giving me.

I talked with John about organising a trip and asked if I could see him. Luckily I had a few days off coming up. Each autumn I tend to plan out the whole of my following year's work; to fit in all of the nursing homes, visits and groups that I go to as a self employed podiatrist, at the frequency they prefer. It's quite a juggle and I create a complicated colour coded timetable; my hand made calendar has been continuous since my school days by repeatedly adding a page at the bottom. But if I see a week when there is very little slotted in, I sometimes leave a few days blank in the hope of taking some time off. I seldom have proper holidays because I don't cope well with being away from home, but enjoy a few days doing something different from time to time. This year there had been a gap at the end of September and

I hadn't made any plans to do anything so it was an ideal time to arrange a visit.

It was fortunate that we hadn't booked time away anywhere else because it was obvious now that this few free days should be spent in Gateshead; I discussed a visit for that week. John was very happy to have me visit and I agreed to phone back in a few days once it was all organised and a hotel booked.

Meanwhile I needed to make sure that my list of memories was as complete as possible and mark what I had got right so far. It was a short life so I was very aware that the details were limited. I also needed to see what I might have got wrong and determine which memories were definitely from childhood recall.

A couple of things that came up in hypnosis initially appeared to be quite wrong. I gave a name Raymond, which I was never certain about. But on a subsequent phone call, just prior to the visit, John told me that his best friend, who was present at the time of the accident, was called Raymond. This was someone John remained in contact with until his death a few years ago. John and his friend Raymond had both been close by when the accident happened and Raymond was also one of the boys Charles also played with. This means that the name did have relevance after all which might be why it seemed clear.

I felt that Charles at the age of six had been learning to read and had a fascination with letters. So the NE also described under hypnosis may have related to Newcastle, and there were the letters seen on the road sign that I picked out, 'e' and 'll', Although I tried many combinations of road name prior to searching records, once I had the address on the death certificate it was clear that it matched Elliott Road very well.

It turned out that I had been trying too hard to use location as the way to solve the memory, when all along the name Charles and the year of death were enough.

Under hypnosis I gave the dates 1939/40-45. Certificates showed the birth to be on the 9th September 1939 and the death on the 19th October 1945, so the years turned out to be pretty accurate. Afterwards I drew out a street plan showing one road almost opposite going away slightly to the right, and remembering walking down our road after turning left out of the house, to get to school. Then crossing the road at the end, turning right, and the school was on the left of that road. This detail felt so confident that I thought it must have always been with me.

John told me that the route to the school was correct, but the school was on the right not the left. Later I realised that he meant you had to turn to the right after crossing over the road at the end, which is what I had said and was indeed where the school used to be. It was a confusing thing at first but at least we were in agreement.

After hypnosis a few memories became clearer, probably because it had given me some detail to concentrate on. The more you remember an event or place the easier it is to remember. The memory becomes a well worn road. It's like practising any skill, like learning to drive for example, the more you do it the easier it becomes until it eventually reaches a point where things like changing gear become second nature. We are made to improve with practice.

I said that the house had a gap to its left where it was not attached to another house; it was a double fronted house and there was maybe one tree and large bushes on the left side. By concentrating I could see the trees and bushes and knew I would be able to describe them to John. All of these things had been found to be correct. There were bushes; John now told me over the phone that there were lots of large bushes at the left side of the house.

I also recalled outbuildings at the side of the house, one of which John told me was told was an Anderson shelter, and I remembered playing at the side of the house or in front rather than in the back garden and wondered if there had been vegetables grown in the garden making it unsuitable for playing in. When I asked John about this he agreed that from time to time his mother grew vegetables and they mostly played in front of the house or in the Anderson shelter at the side.

John told me that there was a lady who lived opposite where the accident happened, who was in her 80's and still living in the same house. It was her mother who took the driver in and looked after him after the accident. I was glad to hear that someone did as it must have been a terrible shock for him. John was finding people who might remember something. He was being very helpful, organised and logical. I then realised this might have been the lady the current resident of the house in Elliott Road had referred to and realised how much easier it could have been if I had contacted her.

I did wonder about the driver of the van. He wouldn't still be alive surely. I wished I could help him to forgive himself and let go of his past pain caused by the accident. I thought about it; the accident was in 1945 so if the driver was fairly young at the time he could be in his late 80's or early 90's. But I didn't know who he was. Without a newspaper article there was no way of finding out. It did occur to me that during the accident my feet would have been sticking out by the back of the lorry on the driver's side, and wondered why the driver didn't see them but his mirrors maybe didn't show his back wheel.

There were a few things to check with John. I made a note to ask him what was opposite the school, something drew my attention. Maybe a shop or something else interesting. I could also sketch the inside layout of the house; John lived there until he was 16 so knew it well. It would be another area to compare for confirmation as I seemed to recall a few details from my dreams of the house over many years.

Having booked a bed and breakfast hotel a little to the south of Gateshead for Saturday September 29th I called John to confirm this date with him. Luckily this meant I now had only a week to wait, which meant there was less time to worry about it.

Fortunately my husband Steve had agreed to drive up with me; he quite liked the idea of a weekend away too. I really didn't want to drive up on my own and was happy to have the company. Steve used to be a haulage driver so prefers to do the driving, which was also helpful as I don't enjoy driving very long distances. Though Steve didn't find my car seats very comfortable for long journeys; but it was either my car or his work van, and the car we had at that time was better for long trips than his old van.

We had decided to make a long weekend of it, taking in a few sights during our return journey. Steve wanted to visit Beamish Museum, where historical buildings are preserved as villages in a 19th century setting, and I always enjoyed seeing the sea, so I hoped to persuade him to detour along the coast on the way back.

As soon as we had decided to go we both came down with a virus. We were just getting over that when, as if to conspire against us the weather took a turn for the worse. The North East was flooding after heavy rainfall; trains had been cancelled and on the radio it said that the main A1 into Gateshead was closed. By all accounts Gateshead and Newcastle were cut off from the south. I also heard on the radio that schools were closed and people were advised not to travel.

But it was only September 25th so it had four days to subside. I wasn't considering cancelling any plans, so packed anyway. It rained again the next day and flood warnings remained in place.

I had predicted problems with global warming, extensive flooding and the spread of monsoon type weather, at least across Britain, back in the 1960s. I even met a dowser at a party in the late 60s who told me of his own dreams of widespread flooding. We then had a long discussion about our foresight and how similar our predictions were and I often think back to that conversation. But over recent years I had taken no pleasure seeing these predictions coming true. The news was full of people in rural villages wading waist deep in flood water. And in the North East in general, flooding was yet again ruining people's homes, businesses and lives. I hoped that John was living on high ground.

I checked the five day weather forecast for the Newcastle area and it showed dry weather for the next few days, chance enough for the flooding to recede. But I was quite determined that the trip was going to happen regardless.

Towards the end of the week I finished work and went to town to buy a disposable camera. I had a lovely new digital camera that my son had bought for me to replace the old 35ml one that had caused so many problems in both Ireland and Japan when I was searching for my past life families there (I managed to come home from both trips without photographs due to the camera fault) but I wanted back up this time.

The day before the trip was exhausting. Every Friday I spent the day looking after my grandchildren, which I loved, but it could be quite stressful and left me feeling very aware of my age and my limits. By the end of the day I was tired and not entirely ready for my adventure.

Chapter 4

Going Home

The drive up to Gateshead took about four hours, without any road hold ups, despite negative messages early on along the motorway suggesting that we might have to detour off the A1.
On reaching Gateshead we drove past the inspiring Angel of the North, I was quite excited to have seen it and rather wished that we had been able to stop and look at it up close; another time maybe. We then followed my carefully photocopied, enlarged and laminated street map that had been pieced together from several pages of the street map book of Gateshead (a new one not the very old out of date one) in order to make directions easier to follow.
The laminated street map might seem somewhat OCD, but the places we were going to, John's home and the old house in Elliott Road, were both on the edges of different pages which would have meant flicking through a map book whilst the car was on the move; a very good way to get lost. The enlargement helped me too, since my reading glasses had to be quite strong these days. Laminating just meant that I intended to make the trip again and wanted that map to last.
John lived only moments from the main A1 so we were soon close by, but we were a bit early. Both of us like to leave early enough to get to places but we had over estimated how long the journey would take. At least arriving early gave us a chance to stop for some lunch and be certain of arriving rested, rather than tired from the journey.
After our break we drove through the last few streets we arrived and parked in the small cul-de-sac, then turned to walk to the bungalow. I noticed that John was already at the open front door preparing to greet us both with a warm handshake and a hearty smile, followed by his wife Isobel. We stared to talk immediately and it was clear that this was going to be a relaxed discussion.

We talked about the film of 'Yesterday's Children' which I had sent to John and he had watched. I'd warned John beforehand by phone that the first ten minutes were a bit confusing because the film was a drama and not factual. The writers had changed my name; nationality; profession, age, family names and family set up. And they had changed the way the memories presented themselves; I would never have crashed the car because I was zoned out. Also I didn't ever forget the memories. In the film the childhood memories had been forgotten but suddenly started to return; this is not what happened.

Perhaps to create a bit of drama the film also added conflict to the level of acceptance of both my family and Sonny Sutton that just wasn't there in reality. But the film was still a good way of explaining what happened and some of the scenes relating to Mary's life with the children were very accurate, which was why I had sent John my copy and why I had also bought myself a replacement copy. There were several scenes that were so true to life that they took me back with tears or laughter. I loved watching the depiction of the children playing with the mattress, stuffing it with fresh wheat chaff and falling about giggling because it was then too big to get back through the door. That scene had been depicted very much as I had remembered it.

John said 'I see what you mean about the film'. But watching it had helped him to understand what this whole thing was about and he seemed very comfortable telling me what happened after his brother Charlie had died.

On the day of the accident John was four years old and was playing with his best friend Raymond in the clay in a front garden about three houses down the road from his home. He heard a lot of screaming and shouting on the other side of the road, directly opposite, and people tried to keep him and the other children from going across to see what had happened.

But people were talking so he soon knew, and he went back home. There everyone was crying, and when they saw him they just cried more. He didn't understand why his standing there should make them cry more. They got even more upset when he said, in all innocence, that it was all right it wasn't him in the accident it was Charlie. I think he felt difficult about this later as he grew up, but at the time he was a small child unable to comprehend the gravity of the event.

His mother Margaret was also about to be remarried. Her first husband, who was also called Charles, had died three years earlier on active duty in Cairo, Egypt. But because he had died in a tram accident rather than in battle, his wife had to fight for a long time to get her widow's pension. She fought with a determination that I could clearly identify with and I mentioned to John that I understood the notion of never giving up. Now she had lost her first son too, again in a road accident. It must have been a terrible day for her.

When I was searching for my family in Ireland a very kind priest helped me find baptism records which made it possible to start to trace the children. He had accepted my memories of the family within the framework of his own beliefs rather than as reincarnation, but wondered what help it would be to the family if I found them.

The priest's words at that time made me think more carefully about my role when stepping into people's lives. I was already cautious not to cause stress if at all possible, but after this, made certain that I always thought about my responsibility to be helpful. I didn't always get it right, but I tried hard to do so. The priests' consideration and thoughtful comments helped me and I will always remember his kindness. So it was a shock when John told me about the priest who spoke to his mother, who was anything but kind.

When Charles was laid out, the priest pointed at the coffin and said to his mother 'That is your fault, it's because you are marrying a protestant'.

To make things worse, after the marriage Margaret's new husband was difficult; he wanted no reminder that Margaret had ever been married before. That included the fact that she had children in her first marriage. When Margaret and her new husband William left Elliott Road and moved into their own home, John was not allowed to go with them. William didn't want the boy in his house. So even though John was still very young, he was left with his grandmother, very much against his mother's own wishes. So John not only lost his brother but he as good as lost his mother as well. His contact with his mother over the years was to be very limited until he was an adult.

Margaret only had one photograph of her son Charles, which she had professionally coloured and placed in a brooch which she wore. But to her husband that was just provocation, it seems, because one day he lost his temper and took it from her and threw it into the fire. He also destroyed all reminders of her first husband, including his medals and any photographs.

This meant that John too had no photographs to remind him of his father or brother, though it may have helped a little that an aunt told him he looked just like his father. But he did have a photograph of his grandmother, a loving and caring woman who was happy to bring him up. I was given a copy of the photo of his grandmother, with one of John's young cousins standing next to her. John had stayed with his grandmother in the house where he was born in until he was sixteen.

Then one day when John had reached sixteen, he was visiting his mother. He had bought himself a smart suit and fashionable high-neck shirt and was sitting with his mother at the table. His stepfather William came in and had been drinking. He taunted John saying 'Are you trying to protect her then'. When John stood up William went for John, grabbing at his throat and he tore the new shirt. John hit him, and hit him again until there was blood on his new clothes.

The police were called and they were about to take John away with them, but John talked to them very calmly telling them his side of the story. The police then turned to his stepfather William and asked for his version of events, but were treated to a shower of abuse. They then realised that John was not the aggressor and he was not in any trouble for the fight. John described this as the last time his step-father ever hurt or threatened his mother.

We did talk about the accident some more. When John asked me what I was looking for I explained that what I wanted was peace. I told John about all of the memories I had with me from childhood; those of Mary Sutton, and about my search in Japan, and how finding the families and places had helped. I also told him about the hypnosis and how it had proven useful in releasing more fragments of memories, though Charles's accident was never explored under hypnosis and the memory in total only revisited very briefly.

Then I told him in more detail about my memory of the crush injury and that this memory had always been with me and came back from time to time. I went on to say that for the whole of this year I had woken with this memory of the accident. I indicated that there was some impact to my right side first, but then drew my hand across my legs just below the knee at a slight angle to indicate where I felt the wheel had passed across the legs. I told him that there was no pain in the memory; John mentioned that shock may have stopped any pain at the time of the accident and I agreed; that was the most likely reason. I told him that there was just time for surprise then it was over.

Several times I apologised that I couldn't remember a lot of detail in general, and that there would be a few mistakes. I told him that I always try to put in the mistakes when I write about it or talk about it because it is right to do so. I said that there was no point doing any of this unless I was as honest and as detailed about the memories as possible. This was before I had been diagnosed so I was unaware at the time that this was another Asperger's trait. Meanwhile John was sitting, quite relaxed and weighing it all up as I talked. His wife, who had by then brought in tea and biscuits, was sitting attentively at his side.

I'd forgotten to bring in my sketch pad in from the car. I always seem to travel with a heap of stuff so it probably got left on the floor, but Isobel kindly found a pad of paper for me. I then sketched the downstairs of the house saying I couldn't remember upstairs. I talked about being ill in a bed in the downstairs room at the front left of the house, maybe with 'flu or mumps, and being looked after by a very kind lady for whom nothing was too much trouble. John said with absolute certainty that it was his grandmother. She helped anyone; she even did the laying out for people (preparing the body when someone had died).

John also told me that the front room I described was the downstairs bedroom, making sense of my remembering being in bed there. I marked a large X and said 'What was there?' and he said that was where the bed was, against the wall. Only later did I realise that if I didn't remember upstairs, and I did remember being in bed set in that room, then the place I'd marked in the corner, the important something that I remembered and wanted to know more about, was probably Charles's brother John. I remembered my bed being in the middle of the room so it was John's bed that was against the wall where I had marked the X.

I described the kitchen as being mostly built across the back wall on the left side of the house and having big cupboards, with which John agreed. Where I marked one area saying that I was sure it was a large walk-in larder he told me that I was right, there was a pantry there, but it was set sideways, longer against the wall than I had drawn. He then said there were several cupboards including a very large gas cupboard. He drew this in on my sketch at the other end of the room to the pantry. I talked about a door with slats of wood like cladding; he told me that was the gas cupboard door.

I had been uncertain whether the kitchen door was in the side or the back but knew it was possible to walk up the left side of the house. When I referred to this as a side access John corrected me. There was no side access, only a window to the pantry and a coal chute. In other words the left side could be accessed to deliver coal and to reach the back garden, but there was no side door. The second door was at the back of the houses, but was indeed accessed by the left side of the house. The other door I remembered seeing at the side of the kitchen was the pantry door.

I said that the right side of the house wasn't clear to me. I had the feeling it was a front room but said that I wondered if it was the parent's room that was perhaps private in some way. He told me it was the main living room that everyone used and went from the front of the house to the back; but that his grandmother slept in there, hence, I assumed, my sense that it was somehow private. I thought that both grandparents slept there but it wasn't until some time later that I confirmed that Charles and John's grandfather John Bryson lived until 1944, so I had remembered correctly. Charles would have been five when he died but John was only three so may not have remembered him.

Several of the grandmother's own children, were still living at home, so I presumed that they slept upstairs which would be why I couldn't remember upstairs. It was being used as bedrooms for the rest of the family so there would have been no reason to have gone up there. The youngest uncle was only ten years older than Charles so the house was full of children and teenagers.

When John described the awful, offhand way he was treated by the hospital when his grandmother died, he mentioned that there were still several of his grandmother's grown children living at home. John told me that neither he, nor any of his grandmother's children were informed by the hospital of their mother's death. There seemed to be no explanation as to why. This was in 1965 when John was 25.

He showed me two photographs of the big black cast-iron fireplace that used to be in the living room, in the hope that I could remember it; it had a large oven one end that was used at Christmas. He let me keep the photographs. John asked if I remembered cleaning the fireplace. I apologised saying that I thought that I didn't, however, I remembered cleaning a very similar fireplace in the cottage in Ireland in Mary's life. So I wondered if sometimes I may have been remembering either or both fireplaces from each life at the same time. There would be no way of knowing, because traditional black fireplaces were very similar the memories of cleaning them would be similar too.

Indeed I have seen cast iron fireplaces in many homes, particularly when I first started working for the NHS back in the 1970s and visited elderly people in their homes. Many homes then had not been modernised and still had the old cooking range; some still had gas lighting and most had open fires. I was always a little sad that our own cottage had the range removed and the kitchen chimney blocked before we bought it; I have always had an affinity for the old style black cast iron range.

John told me that there was a large hearth plinth around the fireplace that the boys used to sit on. I could picture this but couldn't really say that it was a certain memory.

John mentioned that people sometimes thought that he and his brothers were twins because their mother dressed them alike (the grandmother had several sets of twins so may have encouraged it). So I said that they must have looked alike if people thought that. This gave me some idea of how Charles might have looked had he lived, and I found myself looking at John and wondering how I would have looked and what my life would have been like if I had not had the accident. It's a strange thing perhaps but it is inevitable that we wonder what it could have been like to have continued in a life we remember; a 'what if' scenario.

I looked at John to see if I could find any echo of Charles's face and realised that they had both had dark hair. I had dark hair. I had always known Charles had dark hair but foolishly forgot to note it down. Then, coincidentally, just at that moment John's wife Isobel asked what colour hair Charlie had, John and I both said dark, at the same moment in unison, and then cast a glance at each other and grinned. I then added that if he had said blond I would have been very confused.

Then John said something odd, he touched his white hair and jokingly said 'I'm going blond'. It was only odd because that is exactly, word for word, gesture for gesture, what I say about myself and what I have said from when the first white hair appeared. Because it's not something I had heard other people saying about their hair going white I wondered if it was a family thing; perhaps something the grandmother used to say. I was pretty sure it was the first time I had heard anyone other than myself saying this.

John looked at me for a moment and then said, you remind me a bit of my aunt, your hair is exactly the same. But I had for several days before the trip been thinking about someone in the family who had a thick thatch of hair like mine but really couldn't think who it might be.

John had promised to take me to the house and show me where the accident happened. So we all bundled into the car, and I hurriedly took out the remaining child seat and put it in the boot to make room. Lazily I had only taken one child seat out before the trip. John directed us through the easiest route and we were soon at Elliott Road; it wasn't far.

Lots had changed. We parked outside the house but Steve soon had to move the car because there was a tight turn and it was on a bus route. John chatted to the owner of the house who was at his door by now because we had parked outside and were milling about, but also because a bus had come around the corner. The house owner had come out to suggest we move the car, but very politely.

John had a chat with the house owner giving his name and saying that he used to live there and I was doing a story about it.

I looked opposite the house and said to John that the road layout had changed, and I was sure there was a small road just 'here' opposite the house and at an angle; I indicated with both hands where the road used to be. John pointed to the same area, between some new housing, and said 'Yes there was a lane just there' where I had expected it to be. I was relieved. The layout had changed quite a bit and I was very concerned about getting the detail right. My concern was partly because with this memory the detail was limited because it was such a brief life so every tiny little thing counted.

John and I talked about the house a bit. It was very much as I had remembered but looked so much smaller. Of course I was looking at it as an adult and not as a six-year-old boy, it would look smaller, but it still took me by surprise. That is one of the things about remembering a past life. Your memory is as it was from the day of death, it doesn't change. But everything else is constantly changing. So going back is very like returning to your home town many years after you left. What you notice is the differences.

The hedges that used to be down the left side of the house, and which were now absent, were privet, John told me, but they used to be large, overgrown and straggly. That was good; I couldn't recall a neatly trimmed hedge but one that towered above us and had cobwebs we would break with a stick. John remembered the game with the cobwebs but said he and his brother also used to snap of bits of twig and push into the tops of the iron railings.

When he spoke later of toy tanks they played with, I suddenly vividly recalled a solid wooden toy, and was able to describe it and indicate the size. John agreed the description but said they had wheels that went round; and his had a small door on the back that was covered in chocolate. They played on the green area next to the house on the left, where the Anderson shelter was situated. I looked at the green area; it too looked much smaller than I had remembered.

It was a bit confusing though, because so much had been altered. John took me a very short distance, a few doors down, to where the accident happened. It was opposite where he and his friend were playing in the garden. The part of the road where the accident had taken place was now closed off and grassed over, cutting the original road in two. But when it had been part of the road there was also a driveway to someone's house. Where the driveway used to be was now a neat lawn edged with a low rail. This was where the milk float driver reversed and where Charles fell. I stood there and felt wobbly. Not emotional, it was more like unsteady, dizzy; odd. I walked across the same bit of pavement over and over and the odd feeling seemed to turn on and then off again as I passed the spot; it was curious and possibly just because I knew where I was standing. It is very strange to be standing somewhere you remembered dying. There is really no possible description for the curious sensation.

John and his wife stood on the spot for me to take a picture, but somehow the photo I took had John almost off-shot and Isobel completely out of shot, I think I was taken off guard slightly by being at the scene of the accident and not making a good job of the photo opportunities. This is par for me, I would never have made a photographer; I concentrate on the wrong details too much to take a good picture.

While I walked about and took a photo or two of the area John popped into the house to see his old friend; the daughter of the lady who had taken the driver in after the accident; Raymond's sister, still living in the same house after all these years. I realised afterwards that I probably should have gone over and said hello, but was preoccupied with the accident site and hoping that the dizzy feeling might be the precursor of a letting go of the past, or maybe of more memories. It's easy in retrospect to think about what you should have done. I think I would like to have met the lady.

John apologised for chatting with his friend saying he hadn't seen her for a year or so. I said 'Don't apologise', and wondered if we should stay longer, but everyone seemed ready to move on. We had to turn the car around in quite a tight place and find our way back onto the lower section of Elliott Road by a circuitous route, because of all the traffic calming road changes. This meant that we didn't go the way I remembered walking, but I still knew my way around these few streets.

John and I directed Steve towards the school, both at the same time. We rejoined Elliott Road and went down past where the road sign used to be; the one at the bottom of the road where I recalled tracing the letter L twice with my finger. There was no road sign now, probably because there was now a driveway to the last house where the sign used to stand. Then we went right at the bottom of the road and stopped where the school used to be, across the road and just around the corner.

There was still a sweeping opening and iron railings, but no school, just a group of low office-style buildings. The end of that road was now blocked and filled with a few bungalows, whereas it used to have an open access to the next road.

While we had been at John's house I asked what was opposite the school because I was sure there was something interesting, and he had told me there were a few shops, a baker, a chip shop and one other perhaps. That made sense; food shops were interesting to a small boy, especially ones with chips or cakes.

Now we were at the site of the school we could see that the shops had gone too. If I hadn't had John to guide me I could still have found my way about and would still know where the school had been, but with his help I was able to complete the picture and see it all as it had once been.

We returned to John's home and talked some more. John told me that his mother Margaret would have been quite comfortable with the idea of my memories, though I was still not sure. His mother had several meetings with psychics and on one occasion was told that a deceased lady was telling the psychic that Margaret had her wedding ring, the one from her second marriage. Later Margaret had a conversation with her sister-in-law, who had been given money to buy a ring. Apparently she had decided to save money and bought it from a pawn broker, so the ring was indeed second-hand. After that Margaret threw the ring away.

It was too late for me to wonder if I should have searched for Margaret after all. The chance had gone. Now I regretted that I had been so slow to start researching. Margaret died in 1999. There was every opportunity to have found her if only I hadn't procrastinated for so long. I found Charles's birth certificate some years before Margaret died but only got around to ordering Charles's death certificate, where I discovered the address in Elliott Road, in 2002. And it wasn't until 2005 that I wrote to the current house owner; all too late.

As the afternoon progressed we chatted some more and were eventually joined by John and Isobel's son and several of their granddaughters. Not wishing to be in the way we thought it probably was time to leave, if only to free up some of the seating. In a later phone call John said we needn't have rushed off, and I rather wished we hadn't.

We left John's house as the next wave of family, another grand-daughter with two lovely small white dogs, was just coming in. So we were greeting the dogs and all of the family on our way out. John lingered at the garden gate as we left and I was suddenly overcome with the feeling that I had found my brother and didn't want to leave. I knew it was not a journey I could do often and I was saddened by this.

It was later that a few more things fell into place. I remembered walking to school with the mother only, just the two of us. But of course there was a grandmother at home and several of her older children, so there was no need for John to walk to the school and back just because his brother was going.

I recalled what the priest had said to me when I wanted to find Mary's children; 'What help could you be to them now'? In the end the purpose that time, with my family from Malahide and beyond my own need for resolution, was to reunite the family and help them resolve their own past. I wondered what help I was meant to be giving this time. I knew it would help me, but I now felt that this should be about John. Whatever resolution there might be, it was certainly not just about me.

Gateshead was a very long drive away, so any visit would mean at least one overnight stop. But I was already thinking about when we might go again.

Chapter 5

Time to let go

In the first few days after I got home I wrote up as much as I could remember of my meeting with John. He had said I could use all of the names and didn't seem at all bothered by the strangeness of it all. Indeed John's easy going acceptance had made the whole reunion so much better than it might have been.

I woke up the next morning still with the memory of my legs being crushed as I had so many mornings, but now it seemed diminished. I hoped that was because I'd managed to start to resolve everything about the memory and that it might eventually stop. Yet because I'd been thinking about the whole episode for a while, I dwelt on it more whilst awake and it felt more detailed. The time-frame telegraphed.

Repeatedly I went over the memory of the accident. I was obsessed with repeating those few moments over and again. I kept seeing myself lying on the path relatively unhurt; now understanding that it was having fallen from the back of the milk lorry, but feeling a bit bruised on my right side from the fall and maybe winded or stunned. I seemed to be just lying there for a moment which made me wonder if I'd been a bit quicker it might have been possible to get up. I went over the possibilities of survival, such a pointless thought, but inevitable. Again I envisaged my legs being crushed under a wheel and found myself concentrating on the detail. I felt the surprise and looked up and tried perhaps to get up, a little too late. And there it ended. I was trying as hard as I could to see more, to understand, but it always ended at the same place with nothing more.

I now knew that the milk float was reversing at this point, and the driver was unaware of the child lying on the pavement. But the lower part of the legs going under the wheel is the only injury I have ever remembered and has been consistent since early childhood. Try as I might I couldn't recall anything more after this so have to assume that some part of the underside of the lorry then struck the head. This might explain why the memory completely stopped just after the crush injury. I wanted to let go of this silly mental repetition of something I couldn't change.

There never had been memory past this point however hard I tried. And I kept trying. I didn't recall a post death out of body experience as much as I wanted to. Yet I always remembered a post death episode when dying as Mary Sutton. I recalled being high above the body, a little off to one side. I saw a nurse come in then suddenly rush out. Then a priest came and knelt. At that point I was pulled away backwards.

From my life as the Hanafusa girl in Japan I remember being in the water and following a swirling vortex. But I didn't have any more from the life as Charles. This might be because it was so fast and such a surprise. It was a disappointment that the after death out of body experience was missing from this memory but it clearly was; I couldn't summon any recall. I needed to let it go.

I put together some of the paperwork about the family history that Teresa had sent to me and a copy of the family tree updated as far as possible. I wanted to send this to John along with a copy of the section I had written about our meeting, so that he could check it.

The bulk of the family history details are not included here. These are private and nothing to do with the story, but they had been necessary in order to find John and to be sure that he was the right person before I tried approaching him.

I did need to feel that John was happy with what I had written and to make sure it was accurate so I phoned to talk about it. Actually I wanted to phone, and the details of the account were a useful staring point for the conversation. I wanted to check a few extra details too; I wondered which aunts and uncles still lived at home when he was young.

When I phoned John that Wednesday evening he told me that when the photo of his grandmother was taken with his cousin, a second photo was taken on the same day with him in it; it was the only photo of John as a boy, but it had been given to an aunt. John hadn't a single photo of himself as a child. I said he must ask the aunt's family; he was entitled to have a photo, some record of his childhood, but I don't think he ever got to see the photograph.

As we spoke I realised I was right about the reason I couldn't remember going upstairs in the house, because the rest of the family slept there. Although John slept upstairs when he was older, because the downstairs room was quite cold, he told me he was born in the downstairs room and he slept there throughout childhood.

When I checked the dates I realised that when Charles died there would also have been living at home an uncle and aunt who were twins and only fourteen years old at the time, and a sixteen-year-old uncle. The other uncles and aunts were all older so may have left by then.

Charles was born at a different address in 1939, as I had already discovered from the birth certificate, but I discovered that Margaret had to move back home with her parents and siblings when her husband was called up for service at the start of the war; which was pretty much what I had surmised.

John was born in 1941 in the house at Elliott Road a year before his father died. Margaret and her brothers and sisters slept in the upstairs rooms. The grandparents slept in the living room. The boys had the downstairs room. I remembered Charles's bed being in the middle of the room and John remembered his bed being against the wall. Although my memory of John's bed was incomplete I did know that there was importance about that position.

Within the week I was beginning to wake some days without remembering the crush injury at all. I was hoping that this meant the healing process had begun.

The ninth of October was a strange day. I awoke with a sensation of repeated traces across my legs at the same place as the crush injuries but this time lighter, but over and over again. I wondered what I was meant to do. Later at work in a nursing home, one of my patients had the television on and there was a program about the emergency services. A woman had been run over by her own car and was stuck underneath; one wheel had crushed her leg and they had to raise the car carefully to free her.

Being reminded of Charles's accident by this programme left me feeling annoyed. I was once again going through a few 'what if' scenarios and wondered how different things could have been if the driver had stopped and realised there was something wrong or if I as Charles had managed to jump up quickly after the fall. Would there still have been an accident? Could Charles have been saved, might he still be here? It was confusing; I realised that I was angry at the loss of that life but at the same time protective of the life I have now. In many ways I was going through the stages of bereavement. This is quite a normal part of the process after tracing a past life family; wondering what could have happened if things had been different and feeling a bit cheated out of the life lost.

The programme might have been a trigger to opening up more suppressed feelings because later in the day I felt the full force of the grief; of that loss in all its complication. Vulnerability left me feeling washed out and the stress caused my back to seize for the first time in years. It lasted quite a few days and made it pretty well impossible to drive. Every time I tried to get into the car or depress the clutch my back went rigid in spasm and I couldn't move; so I had to have time off work for the first time in many years.

By using a tight wide belt holding the spine firmly to reduce movement the pain was controlled a bit. But I had to sleep on my right side where shoulder ligaments I had torn a few months earlier caused even more pain. Plenty of back exercises and keeping as mobile as possible corrected the problem in a week or so. I am unable to take pain killers due to my allergies, but the pain of the muscle spasms seemed an irrelevant inconvenience in comparison with the grief.

When it hits you, the real sense of loss of a life you should have had but one that was cut short, overlaid by the knowledge that without that loss the present would be so very different, it is difficult. Mixed with the sense of loss of self was also guilt at having brought the whole past life package to the door of the person most important in the search, in this case John, Charles's brother.

I'd experienced this process before when I found my family in Ireland, but was less prepared then. That time I found it difficult to understand what I was going through and it got in the way of everything. It surprised me. I had found my children from the life where I had died as a young mother and been separated from them. The past had happened and the present had caught up. But the confusion caused by conflicting emotions from the two different lives and two sets of memories was emotionally immobilising. Indeed the stress was great enough to trigger allergic responses; I suddenly found that alcohol or chocolate could cause life threatening anaphylaxis.

The stress passed in due course though annoyingly the severe allergies remained. Spending time with my Irish family helped get everything into perspective and slowly I let go and was able to see both lives without the weird sense of emotional dichotomy.

But that was almost twenty years earlier. Since then I had looked at a number of my past lives and confirmed quite a bit of detail of several, especially about the Japanese life. I had searched, found and in the main had been able to move on. I was very aware that it wasn't a smooth process. So this time I was well aware how emotional it could get and knew that the best way to cope with past life grief, as with any grief, was to let it run its course and allow whatever feelings arose to do what they need to do. It would pass.

There is never any going back. And now my life was so full of love, my grown children, my grandchildren; all part of this life that I couldn't have had without losing the one before when I did. But I had been lucky, amazingly lucky because in some way, by finding my way back I could have a bit of that last life once again; a connection. In this way I could almost have both lives and all of the other lives I had lost and found, all at the same time.

Nobody warns you about this, probably because the researches are one step removed from the feelings involved and quite possibly unaware of the emotional Pandora's box opened by this kind of exploration. Most people who experience past life memories are children, so perhaps they are not as vocal or as able to tease apart the feeling or express them completely. But it is a bitter-sweet moment; and so difficult to explain. So I tried to explain it and write about it whilst it was still fresh and raw; because we soon forget grief as the intensity wanes.

Although I had looked at many past lives this was only my second time around with finding a living contemporary relative. This means someone who could remember from their current life what I could remember from a past life; someone who was there. Being able to complete past life research and meet face to face with people who I knew before was an uncommon experience. Time had allowed me to explore the feelings, yet it was still a bit of a surprise when it hit home so hard.

Now I knew why I had avoided concentrating on this memory for so long. I even let myself become detoured with a long past memory, discussed in a later chapter, when I should have been looking into Charles. And now that I had found the time, courage and good fortune to complete the search I knew why I had been writing so fervently, so obsessively, every spare moment since the visit to Gateshead. It was in the hope that the activity could in some way ameliorate the sense of loss. But then in the midst of grief there was also joy. When I looked at it properly I realised that I had the best of both worlds.

Things had changed again. Now I had contact with a brother who had been lost to me through the terribly sad death of a child. I had the chance to see the home I remembered and to talk about the family I had lost. My fragmented recollection felt repaired, I was connected again.

With Mary's life and memories it had been the same, at times the competing emotions had been hard to understand; but I had my family back. Now, even though Mary's children had all gone now, I still very much appreciated the contact I had with some of Mary's extended family. I had re-found the people I had

67

loved in the past, and was still surrounded by the family and friends I loved in my present life. Yes it was complicated, but it was also magnificent.

Now I had revisited another life. This time around it was almost as if I had stepped from that life to this with little change. There was a gender change, but I was a boyish child so it didn't seem a lot different. I was as fascinated with cobwebs in the privet bushes as Charles was, though I did grow out of poking them with a stick. As a child I sought outdoor adventures and wore boy's clothes; usually my older brother's hand-me-downs. I realised that this time I hadn't changed very much at all.

For a long time I had wondered about the changes in the transition from life to life. My feeling is that only a subtle core personality is transferred through death and a lot of who we were is just let go. Certainly our mood is controlled by things that would have no place within a spirit existence, like hormones and hunger and even genetics. But it felt as though the similarity moving from the life as Charles to my current life was easy, so now I wasn't sure. That child, Charles, was me even more than Mary Sutton was me. Of course it was more recent, this could be why, but I continued to find the sense of sameness intriguing.

Towards the end of October I spoke to John again and he said something that made everything right. He told me that he felt connected. He was quite young when his brother died, and it was so long ago but now, through me, he felt as though he was connected to his brother again. This was what I lived for. I thanked him. I said that I was sure he would tell me exactly what he thought any time and I was good with that, I like direct people. So did he; we were off to a good start.

Over the years that followed John and I spoke on the phone regularly and Steve and I visited John and Isobel in Gateshead quite a few times. We would drive up for a long weekend and visit for the Saturday. Steve and I would then take our time getting back and see areas of the country that interested us on the way home.

We slipped into a comfortable easy friendship and I was grateful that it had all worked out so well. It is possible to find a past-life family and almost pick up where you left off.

For a few years I still experienced the sensation of my legs being crushed upon waking, but I soon learnt that it was an unconscious nudge encouraging me to do something or a reaction to stress. All I had to do was recognise that I needed to address a problem and get on with it. Instead of being something terrible from a fatal accident it had changed into a subtle alarm system. So I no longer feel distressed when the sensation occurs, it was just telling me to listen to my instincts and do something. It almost stopped but never completely went away. But it was not stressful; in resolving the past I had let go.

Chapter 6

Between lives and other questions

Many of the questions I am asked are to do with what happens to us between lives. I promised my readers that I would try to answer their questions here more fully than is possible via Internet media and was given some extra questions as a response.

The initial stages experienced after death have been well researched, by asking people who have had near death experiences. Due to the skill of modern medicine, increasing numbers of people have been revived from serious incidents and lived to tell the tale.

When I first started to talk about my own memories of between lives, I hadn't read about the stages reported in near death experience. Then at a conference in Norway in June 1994 I was asked what I recalled of the between life time. After my nervous response I was introduced to Dannion Brinkley, a near death survivor, who concurred with pretty much everything I could remember. Dannion then introduced me to Raymond Moody, the first researcher to indicate the stages of post death experience from his research with near death survivors, including Dannion Brinkley.

After death you feel yourself suddenly thrown out of the body, not drifting slowly as some film makers like to imagine. You may find yourself above the body and a bit to one side. The position, of not being directly above, reminds me of refraction in water, as though you are in a different medium to the atmosphere, which seems likely. When leaving Mary Sutton's body I felt that I was at least hospital ceiling height if not more, but could still see the body below me.

Then I seemed to curl up like a small ball of just energy and shot off through something akin to a worm hole, very much like Hollywood depictions of a worm hole this time, with vivid colours like shafts of light all around me. When I died as the

Hanafusa daughter in Japan I was under water and this wormhole effect initially appeared as though a swirling vortex of water.

The next stage is arriving in the place of light. Many near death survivors talk about meeting a relative at this point and experiencing a life review, where you feel the things you have done to others as though done to you. I didn't remember much of this so can't add to it, but I did have a feeling that any punishment was self regulated, that you punish yourself, which does seem to concur with the research.

At this point people who have a near death experience usually return to their bodies, very few see beyond the life review. But the next bit is what I remember most. So the questions I am asked start with 'What is it like?'

Firstly, it is a very different sensation. You have no body so have no physical needs including most of the emotional needs, probably because these are hormone driven, therefore physical. So perhaps the closest analogy would be to think about meditation. In meditation you let go of the physical side and exist in the present as an extended moment. Expand that thought to a constant state and you begin to get the feeling of between lives.

I felt as though I was in a timeless place full of light and in the connected presence of many other souls. Each person was like a ball of energy; the background was very bright with a few blue shafts of light running through it. The individuals weren't all packed in like a ball pit, all touching, nor spaced sparsely like stars in the sky, but set at even spacing; close but loose.

It felt outside of time and the light that stayed on constantly may have been created by the souls themselves or may have been generated by the place itself. The blue strands of light seemed to be part of the place.

There was a sense of being connected to all of the other lives in a very personal way, as though we are all part of a single energy. There was little sense of separation one from another except that we existed each in our own bubble of energy.

A few near death survivors can also recall bright light and some describe what they see as something recognisable, like large white bright buildings. Many understand a sense of connectedness. Those with various religious beliefs tend to describe what they see in terms of their expectation.

Sometimes I have been asked what we do between lives. The answer has already been given, we have no body so have no needs, we are in a state akin to meditation where the moment of now is extended and the state of just being is enough. So the answer is that we don't have a need to do anything. The place feels timeless; there is little sense of time passing so the suspended moment of now has no sense of taking time. In other words you can't get bored if you don't sense time passing. A bubble of life energy has no need to do anything. It is a time to recover, contemplate and rest.

Do we choose who we will be with in our next life? The word 'choose' is a bit of a problem here because we are in a removed state, so my feeling is that any choice is instinctive rather than reasoned. Perhaps the best answer is that we choose in the same way that we might choose who to fall in love with. I do think we are drawn to other people, for whom we feel empathy, or whom we recognise either by their familiarity or by their similarities either to us or to others we have known. So we may select instinctively to allow ourselves to be drawn to someone, or several people, but my feeling is that choice is not direct. Although there are children who talk about distinct choice this might not be usual.

Sometimes people are horrified by the thought that they may have chosen to live with parents who treat them badly, but you need to remember that the selection does not usually seem to be conscious; it is instinctive and subtle. In just the same way you might fall in love with someone who then treats you badly, you can end up with a poor choice of family. In my experience most people in the world are relatively kind given a chance, so sometimes it is just circumstance that turns relationships sour. Often it is due to mental health issues or financial worries, or

72

sometimes that the person who is unkind suffered some sort of abuse in their upbringing that taints their viewpoint.

I was asked if you always return with significant people from past lives. It occurs to me that all of my children from Ireland and my mother and brother from my Gateshead life, couldn't return with me to this current life as they were still already living the lives I remembered them from. I do think we can return to be with people we have known before by being drawn to familiarity. I don't think it will happen every time but it may happen with some regularity.

There are a number of researched cases say that claimants say that they were family members, like a grandparent returning to the same family, or connected in some other way. In strong cases this may be one of the few ways to verify the sense of being drawn to particular individuals. However, returning to the same family seems much less common than to return to a life with someone unrelated.

Do we recognise people in spirit form whom we knew? Many near death survivors say that they are met by a relative or close friend when they first arrive at the place of light. They say they recognise the person. I have no experience of this but it is a consistent claim. I think it likely that we are able to recognise a soul.

How long are we in spirit form? The gap between researched past lives varies from between less than a year, to a dozen years, but around six to eight years seems common. I've checked the gap between my own lives and it was about 20 years between drowning in Japan and being born in Ireland; though that is a long gap and I suspect there could have been a child or baby death in between that which I don't recall, or indeed several. Mary to Charles was eight years and Charles to my current life was another eight years. There is a possible four year gap before Japan. Because the world is now vastly overpopulated I would expect that gap to become much shorter. The shorter gap could add to anxiety as there might be insufficient time spent between lives to recuperate.

73

When I was between lives did I react with other spirits or contemplate my past life? My memory is that all of the thoughts about the past life were during the initial arrival stage along with the life review. After that the memory was less significant until a new body was selected. Reacting with other spirits; forget any thoughts of conversation and think instead of an unspoken moment of connection. Then stretch that moment out and include everyone around you. There was a sense of oneness, but not reacting in a normal communication sense.

Did I think about the people I had left behind? Yes, I'm sure of it. But maybe les so after being on the other side for a while, in the same slightly detached meditative way without emotive reactions like sorrow or anger, just love.

What do I think is the purpose of this state of being between lives? I think it's our true state. I think the purpose of physical being is to experience change and interaction to evolve and feel. Our purpose is fulfilled here but understood there.

Does everyone reincarnate and can we choose not to return? I think that reincarnation is just the way that life works. So all life, all living things would have two forms, one here and the other there. Maybe part of us exists in the between life place all of the time and only part of us comes back in a physical form. I don't think we have much choice about whether to return. Perhaps as the process of evolution continues we might reach a stage where it is no longer necessary to keep returning, but for the system to work it would have to have happened from the very start of life.

Do you come back as the same gender? The answer is no, there is no reason why you should. A lot of people don't realise that apart from the physical differences there is a huge overlap in characteristics, so gender change doesn't usually mean much of

But remember that time has no meaning between lives. My recollection is that all that happens is a subtle change after a while, where a sense of need begins to develop in place of the sense of peace and oneness. But that could be due to the formation of a new body that the soul is already beginning to inhabit.

a shift in personality. Research suggests that the overlap in characteristics is around 40%. So 40% of women have strongly male characteristics and visa versa. That is before any consideration of sexual preference, which is another issue apart.

Professor Ian Stevenson only mentioned having six cases where recalling a previous life in a different gender could have caused gender identity problems. One of these was the case of Ma Tin Aung Myo, a girl born in Burma in 1953 who remembered being a male cook with the Japanese army in Burma killed in an air raid. She always dressed as a boy and when she grew up continued to live as a man and had a female partner.

I didn't recall any problem with gender changes but I was advised by a researcher that some people do develop gender identity issues with changes life to life. It could be because many of my male lives didn't extend into adulthood or it might be that only a small number of people find they have gender dysphoria from past life changes.

Could it be genetic memory rather than reincarnation? Genetic memory suggests that the memory is carried on the DNA. For this to be the case the person would have to be a direct descendant of the person whose life they remember; so their own grandfather for example. Some people do come back into the same family but the majority of cases are people who are not directly related.

I did come across someone who thought that if you had a distant relative in the family who came from the same area you might be genetically related so the memory could jump across. Genetics doesn't work that way. You share sections of DNA with many people you are related to but inheritance travels in a straight line from parents to children, not sideways. Because we are all related to each other we are all connected. It is possible to envisage a sharing of memory via some sort of species telepathic link but the term genetic memory would appear to have no value as a concept.

Someone also wondered whether if we could prove that past life memory was not genetic memory, we would then be proving it was reincarnation. This is of course not the case; all you would be proving is that it isn't genetic memory.

Do we develop in proportion to the effort we put in, or is it a matter of fate, with choices limiting our experiences and therefore our development? I think that the ratio between development and effort tallies. Limited experiences probably don't limit our efforts. I feel strongly that it is the small things in life that make the difference; small kindnesses. So I do think that if we try to be fair and kind we can develop better. In any case it's a good rule for life to try to be kind to each other. Even when making a complaint it is completely possible to do so kindly and with consideration.

Do we have the same finger-prints? We don't retain physical traits to do with genetics; we might also be a different race or gender, so clearly no, we wouldn't. We can however have a similar posture or facial expressions. There is also a whole section of research into birth-marks that identify past life accidents or gunshot wounds or other physical trauma. It is now generally accepted that we can carry a birth mark that has meaning from our previous life, though obviously not all birth marks would be in this category; most are inconsequential.

From different lives we have different names; do we have one name we go by? Names are not important in the long term. 'A rose by any other name would smell as sweet' because of course we are not the name given to us by others. I have no sense of a name between lives and I don't think we need one. Here we need names and they are important to identify each other, but between lives we probably know who we are without the need for a name.

What do people experience as they pass? If a death is sudden there might only be time for surprise, but it is dependent on the manner of death. If you have been lucky enough to sit with someone as they let go you will probably have noticed what people see. Right at the point of letting go people often relax, pain seems to leave them and some mention the light or see someone they knew. There is a brief moment of peace and acceptance and for many people, serenity.

There are other questions I am asked that are more general. Do we have a genetic connection with people we were in a past life? People do seem to come back to the same region, more often than they return to somewhere distant; though that region can be large and it is the area rather than any particular race that they return to. So I connect with France, England and Ireland repeatedly, with just one life in Japan. But there is no necessity for a genetic connection beyond normal chance.

Related to this I am asked if I have any Irish connections in my family that could tie me genetically with Mary Sutton. I think that this is because people look for a genetic link to match the spiritual one. But pretty much every family in England has an Irish great-grandparent. One of my great-grandmothers was a Hogan, but the Hogan family were in Greenwich, London, for generations and I cannot go back far enough to find one who was born in Ireland. However, it would have been before 1800 with my fourth great-grandfather or even further back.

I did have a 24% Celtic result on a DNA test which is often an indication of Irish descent, but it turned out to be mostly Cornish; my father's family originally came from Cornwall. I used to completely dismiss any thoughts about genetic connections in relation to reincarnation because I see the body as a physical vehicle and the spirit as separate, but some researchers have found that there is sometimes a connection of sorts. For one, as previously mentioned, some people come back to their previous family, as their own grandchild or great-grandchild.

The problem I see with looking too hard into genetic connections is that we are all related anyway. There were so few people alive in the distant past that we all share the same relatives. In many ways there might be no more genetic connection from one life to the next than there is between you and your next door neighbour.

What is the purpose of reincarnation? I look at it as the simple mechanics of life; all life. If the process is that life is recycled, then it would always be recycled. It would have to be a constant for every living thing since life began, not just us.

Are we always human or can we come back as an animal? It's probably easier to be human if you have been human before and it is probably easier for other animals to stay the same too. It's easier to adjust to a society if you have had practice in previous societies. And if you have experienced socially evolved, tolerant societies, you are more likely to want to push for change where there is injustice and want your society to be better. It makes sense to come back as what you have been before and use what you have learnt.

As we become more complex animals the process itself may become more complex. What we see as our purpose may be our underlying need to improve, which is part of social evolution. In a way we might take the reins of our own development as we become aware of our ability to do so.

Can we live our lives in any order, out of sequence, or do they follow linear time? I am not sure what benefit there would be to living out of sequence, but also think it to be impossible. One reason is that we live a life, die and spend time in the realm between lives and then return. Some of us remember the sequence and it is as linear as each individual life. There is no disconnect between one life and the next, it's all joined up and going in one direction.

But another reason has to do with space/time and relativity. Simplified, the faster you go through space the faster you go through time, because they are the same thing. So people who went to the moon very fast in a space rocket gained a partial second on us.

Again a simplification, this planet hurtles through space at an amazing speed, something like 483,000 miles per hour. The speed may be what gives us time as we understand it. However, scientists suggest that even if the universe expansion slowed to a stop, subatomic particles would still be moving so time would still exist. But relative time suggests that it would slow. Time is linked to space.

In other words travelling through time is probably impossible but travelling through relative time might be what we do to experience time. But it's always a one-way journey, forwards.

The spirit part of our existence cycle would also have to be connected to us in space-time by some means or we would not be able to return, because the planet would be in a different position; we would have to move with it in time and space.

I am often asked how old I was when I started remembering a past life. The question assumes that I forgot then suddenly started to remember. The question seems to be in error. I started talking about past lives at the age of three because I didn't understand why people didn't talk about their own past lives all of the time. I assumed it was considered impolite. However, as far as I am aware the memories were with me always. So I was about three, going on four, when I first spoke about past lives, but that wasn't when I remembered them; I just didn't forget.

Did I only remember in dreams? No, most of the memories were normal memories, it was only the deaths that were pushed aside and appeared in dreams or upon waking. However, I found it easier in first contact with my Irish family to initially refer to dreams; I thought it was a simpler way to explain in the initial stages. It was important to me to try to make it easy and unproblematic for my past life family as possible, so to start with I just described the dreams and this description seemed to perpetuate.

Do I still remember past lives? The memories remain but once a life has been resolved there is less need to think about it as much so there is a tendency to let go of some of the detail.

Does it make me feel different? There is no reason why it should; we have all had past lives, simply remembering it doesn't make a person different and certainly not special.

In the autumn of 2012 I talked with Brazilian psychotherapist, Julio Peres. He was recording a series of interviews mainly with prominent researchers, Jim Tucker and Erlendur Haraldsson and others, for a course he was involved in. This was to train psychotherapists in reincarnation related matters. I'm no academic, but Julio had asked me to provide a response relating to the role of psychotherapy when someone has a past life memory.

I had met Julio some years earlier at a conference in London that I had attended in order to record an interview for Brazilian book publicity. They had wanted me to travel to Brazil, but it was soon after my trip to Japan and I was reluctant to travel again. I needed down time before considering any more travel so had suggested the recording instead.

Julio asked what symptoms I experienced when I had spontaneous recalled flashes of another life. I had to explain that I had no symptoms as it wasn't a disease and that the memories were not spontaneous flashbacks but normal recall, albeit of a previous life.

Several people have asked me this kind of question and I have to admit I always find it difficult to reply, because remembering a past life doesn't have to be a problem and is certainly not an illness in any sense. But I do understand that when someone seeks professional help it is usually because they do have a problem. Any memory of an event can be the cause of discomfort whether from this life or a previous one. In these circumstances someone might seek help. Sometimes fears or phobias can be related to a past life rather than the current one.

For most of us it's the separation from the past life families that's hard, and the sense of grief. It's possible that the stress of not being able to resolve the past could be rather more problematic than the memory itself. Unfortunately it is not always possible to trace a past life family to gain that degree of closure, though some closure can be attained without full resolution.

The next question was originally going to be 'How did I deal with the symptoms that emerged from my past lives?' But this changed in respect of my previous answer. We talked about people who had contacted me with past life problems. War events have caused terrible stress for many people and it still does. Shell-shock, post-traumatic stress, anger management issues, even alcoholism or violence, all of these things can be caused by living through the horror of war, even if the war occurred in a previous life. I had been contacted by people with some of these problems so understood that it could be a source of anxiety.

The next question asked if there could be a convergence between psychotherapy and reincarnation. I didn't know much about psychotherapy and wasn't quite sure what the question meant, but I do know about talking with people when you are worried about something. And it struck me that a listener, whether friend or professional, should be willing to listen without judging. This ran into the next question, which was asking how psychotherapists could help people going through the same experience. This was far more relevant.

Most people who have past life memory have a few needs in regard to their memory. They need some kind of verification, acceptance and to be able to share with someone. Most feel driven to find their past life family and be reunited. But in the end, as with anything that has gone and is in the long past, there is a need to be able to let go and move on.

Some general verification is often possible; it's just a matter of going through the memories and matching them to history. Absolute verification such as identifying the actual person is harder. But the best option is often just acceptance through talking with others who are completely comfortable with the notion.

Being able to share with like-minded individuals is much easier now with the Internet. There is no need for anyone to feel alone with something that others might not understand. There are many people who remember and want to share their feelings and experiences with others.

The last two questions related to the psychotherapists and what they could do to help. I was asked to offer advice for the psychotherapists on the course. Not exactly my field of expertise but I suggested that perhaps if they were to look at the phenomena as just being memories and treat them the same way they would any other memories, it could be positive. This should be regardless of what views the psychotherapist holds about past life memory. The person in front of them needs respect and needs to feel they can trust the therapist without being judged.

Perhaps the most important thing here is that there is a course set up that psychotherapists are willing to take, to help people come to terms with past life memory. This in itself is a positive move. I have no doubt that some people taking this course might be doing so without any acceptance of the reality of the experience, purely looking at it from a clinical viewpoint. But even thinking about the experience and how best to approach their patients, is a very helpful step forwards.

Chapter 7

Remember

Past life memory is about remembering, but what do we know about memory? Many psychologists seem to agree that we cannot consciously remember anything that happened to us before the age of three and that most people cannot remember events occurring before the age of six. Apparently if we revisit memories or talk with others who were there, our recall of the events can change.

This is because generally the things that have happened to us, events, life experience memory, or autobiographical memory, are believed not to begin development until around the age of two or three and are not properly developed until later.

One problem with autobiographical memory is that it's partly there to help us to prepare to cope with a variety of events that we may have to face in the future, by referring to past experience. Rather than being an accurate record of our personal life history it is thought to be an aid to prediction. This would explain why our memory is sometimes prone to error and alteration. We change things around to see how they would fit into slightly different circumstances that could happen later. This is a bit like the predictive algorithms or predictive analytics used in computing systems, but with a much more random component, imagination.

This same process can be seen in the way we mix up the day's events in strange and novel ways when we dream, in order to assess and collate events as they pertain to our ongoing progress through life. Our dreams are a mishmash of the day's events, because it helps our unconscious make sense of them. Fiction, in the form of television, films and books can become part of this process and help us envisage what we would do if something happened; how we might react to an event. So people might respond instinctively to a crisis because they have already rehearsed it in dreams.

But this is not the whole story. Of course there are many people who have very precise memories from early childhood. And we don't just remember things from our childhood because they have been repeated in family stories; we remember them independently.

Despite the picture given by psychologists, many of us know that it is perfectly possible to remember being a baby. I have talked with a number of people, who like me, are able to remember quite specific events from their early years. We can remember being bathed in the sink and sitting on the draining board with our legs only just long enough to reach into the water. Or sitting in a pram with the safety straps holding us back; we can remember what it was like learning to walk and having to climb steps in a semi-crawl, because our short legs and poor balance made walking up a step too hard. Some of us can remember what it was like to have dirty, scraped hands when we fell while learning to walk. Memory should not be underestimated.

Also memory is not just a reconstruction with alterations to help us predict how to respond to possible future threats. Precise and unchanging memory is just as important for our survival. So it cannot be assumed that all memory is altered by time; clearly it is not. The reason that exact memory aids survival is partly to do with our navigation skills. In a more primitive society, before the written word and before maps, we had to find our way about by memory and it had to be right.

Civilisation didn't really take hold until after the end of the Ice Ages. Until farming began people were all nomadic; we moved over vast territories following animal herds or travelling away from the worst of the weather. The need to remember where fresh water was found in a given area, or fruit bushes or other seasonal food sources, was a matter of life and death; an essential survival tool and therefore very necessary.

So long-term memory that is unaltered when recalled has a significant survival value and must be every bit as important as memory that is juggled around to use for future predictions. Both systems are needed. It is the unaltered memory we look for when researching our past lives; accurate detail rather than imaginative predictive memory.

It is perhaps no coincidence that our internal map, recalling the layout of an area, is high on the detail recalled in past life memory. Because this is precisely the kind of memory that survival has deemed necessary. So remembering the roads and location with a past life memory becomes likely; it's the part of memory that works most accurately.

To further stress the importance of this very exact navigational memory, it's not just humans who need to remember their relative location; it's a survival tool for all animals so is a consistent trait. Elephants need their good memory to find food when weather conditions are unfavourable; the older elephants can lead the herd to where they recall finding food they were taken to in their youth. They travel huge distances and might only cover the same ground a few times in their life. A good and accurate long term recall has to be paramount for finding food and water and consequently to survive during difficult times.

Fish manage to find the spawning grounds where they were born. Salmon swim to the mouth of the river they came from and swim back to the place of their birth. Many varieties of birds migrate across entire continents over the course of a year. Exact memory is essential.

So when I remember a past life it should be no surprise that I can draw maps of the areas where I lived before. I am just taking advantage of a deeply rooted instinct for survival common to us and many other animals. The first thing we do when we go anywhere new is to find our bearings, see where the shops are, make sure we can get back to where we are staying. This might be the most precise and important of all of our memory abilities. So if you find yourself sketching a map of an area you recall from a past life it might be an idea to trust it.

Martin Conway, of City University London, developed experiments that he feels, show that children don't tend to remember an event until they have learnt the words to describe them. This might be generally accurate and clearly this is what the experiments seem to demonstrate, but I cannot entirely agree. Some of us easily remember events from pre-verbal childhood. This seems reasonable if we again look at animals. Most animals have only limited communication, but it doesn't seem to impair their memory at all. Complex language is not a prerequisite for memory even if it is required for sharing what you remember.

An octopus is a very particular example as octopi are known for their curiosity and intelligence. They are abandoned by their mothers and have to rely on their intelligence and their memory, without any communication from parents to help teach them. They do this extraordinarily well without proper language or teaching.

Some of the memories from early childhood can be very detailed and include the whole range of senses. As a baby I was regularly put out on the lawn in a pram, as was the custom, and remember how very lonely and isolated it felt. There is a particular memory of trying to twist around against the harness to gain attention from a passer by. I could hear her heels clicking on the road long before I could see her walking past; but much to my sadness she just walked on.

I remember vividly how it felt. I could smell the grass. I must have only just learnt to sit up because I remember how hard it was to pull myself up. I felt the harness holding me back and felt trapped and frustrated by it, I felt the warmth of the sun but it wasn't on my face. I was hurt that I had been left alone and ignored. It became too tiring to sit up so I collapsed back into the pram and the partial occlusion created by the hood. Past life memories are often similar to this; the whole range of senses, a lot to pick up on.

It's possible that someone who remembers past lives may also remember very early events in their childhood simply because they already have practice at recalling life events. Recalling a past life through early childhood before being able to verbalise, might help to hold the accuracy of the memory intact. So that when a past life is first discussed, the detail could be at its very best and most reliable. This makes a good argument for following cases where small children remember a past life; the accuracy may well be much greater at this stage.

But having a past life memory as a child affects the child. I am certain my childhood was coloured by the awareness that I had been an adult previously. I recall feeling a little humiliated in a number of my very early childhood memories, simply because I was treated as a child. The lack of self determinism was a problem too. Later, perhaps by school age, I realised that children are not treated in the same way as adults and was better able to cope, but it did take time to accept being a child again.

Looking at the connection between people remembering their early childhood easily and remembering a past life, it's interesting that a common method used in regression hypnosis, to help people recall a past life, is to take them first to early childhood memories. If, as I suspect, most small children have some access to previous life memories, then taking a person back to that time may help them know what they knew then. And of course, thinking back to a time when we were very young is only a small step from thinking back to when we were here before.

Under hypnosis I was assisted to recall my birth and the slightly unusual events immediately following my birth, which turned out to be entirely accurate (I asked my mother) so this must have been stored as memory in my brain. We only tried this experiment under hypnosis following a similar experiment, which used a number of people who were asked to recall their own births under hypnosis and all correctly remembered their head position, which was confirmed by hospital records. So I am not at all unique in this; you could probably remember your birth under hypnosis or meditation. This tends to suggest that we can all lay down memories at least from the moment of birth, so in theory should be able to access early memories.

So some of us can remember how we felt about events and the physicality of moving as a small child. Retelling might change the memory of an event but this is not necessarily so. For example, when as a toddler, I was told off for washing my hands in my grandmother's dog's water, and told off again for drinking the freshly replaced water after being specifically told it was drinking water; the story was retold. But my own memory included things like how hard it was to climb the kitchen step from the garden and then noticing how dirty my hands were. I remember how difficult it was to lap water like a dog and how hurtful it was when people laughed, when all I was doing was trying to get things right in my very literal way.

If you are someone who remembers early events then most of the memories from the age of two or under are likely to be ordinary things, like learning to talk properly, potty training, being embarrassed at being changed in front of a stranger. There is probably no difference in quality or detail between memories as a one or two-year-old child or as a ten-year-old, or even as a young adult.

It probably is true that the number of recalled events increase year on year, so that by the age of three to four there is more significant recall. This might be why people think that they don't have early life recall. Then again, brain wave patterns change at around school age which might make remembering pre-school times harder, but not impossible.

John Savage, the brother of my Charles's past life, has very clear memories of his brother and the accident that took Charles's life even though he was only four at the time. I think if we have reason to remember then we will remember. It may well be true that many people don't remember much before the age of six, but it is not a clear-cut thing. I think many more people have early memories than researchers in the field might realise.

So, experiments suggest that we could all recall our own births accurately; or at least the head position if we use hypnosis to help us. Consequently we might lay down detailed memories in our early childhood but not find access easy later. Equally we could all have past life memories that we bring with us but may have the same difficulty accessing those as we do our early childhood. And maybe accessing early childhood memories might also releases past life memories.

What can you do about this on your own? It is probably worth trying to meditate on early memories as a key to opening up to past life memories. As a small child, the most prominent memories will be the events of significance, like birthdays or unusual personal events like a first bee sting. I do feel that it is worthwhile using this route to exercise your memory and open the door to your past. By thinking about your earliest memory and concentrating on the detail you might find it possible to go further back, step by step.

Past life memory is just that, memory. It has to be stored in the brain whilst we have a physical body so it must be possible for everyone to access it in normal ways, even if only a few glimpses. The big problem of course is that past life memory dates back through a period when the spirit had no physical body and therefore no brain to store the memory in.

Memories are made and stored by a physical system, neurons in the brain. So it is puzzling how it could be possible to remember back through many lives over an extended time span when there was no physical vehicle for the memories to exist within. I console myself when I read science journals and realise how little we really understand about anything; even something as apparently simple as gravity seems to evade full definition. Sometimes we just have to accept that as yet, we cannot find an answer. However, I discuss possibilities in a later chapter. Apparently we do carry our memories from life to life so there must be some other mechanism at work than just our physical brain.

Our minds work in many curious ways. Dreams are important; we use both dreams and our passion for fantasy stories, as evidenced by the market for highly imaginative books, television and films. We can view life obliquely in order to organise how we interpret reality; and, as the research shows, to predict how we might respond to future events. By placing the normal into the realms of the bizarre in our dreams, it allows us to explore reality from an indirect angle. This curiously allows us a better grasp of reality and fuller understanding of our own nature.

It was fascinating to discover that people born with paraplegia dream about walking and running about as much as anyone else, and people born deaf dream that they have conversations. The way it happens seemed very like memory to me, and I wondered if people drew on past life memory to experience these dreams.

Alan Hobson of Harvard Medical School and Ursula Voss at Bonn University headed teams collecting dream information from people born with these two disabilities, deafness and paraplegia, as reported in New Scientist 13/8/11. They noted that there was no difference between the number of bodily movements within a dream by someone who was born paraplegic or by someone who was able bodied.

The researchers concluded that dreams tap into representations of movement or conversation and are independent of waking experience.

I would consider past life memory within the explanation. Perhaps people can unconsciously remember living without a disability and therefore dream about themselves without a disability.

I was told about a troublesome dream someone who was deaf from birth had; repeatedly. She was in a war situation with many aircraft diving low overhead and bombing the town she was in. The most frightening thing was the noise. She remembers screaming with her hands over her ears trying to shut out both the noise and the horror. But this terrifying dream made her less bothered about being deaf in this life. Indeed, the dream was the reason she gave for refusing a cochlear implant when she was offered the surgery. She had no desire to be able to hear, even if it could make life easier.

Dreams are important for our mental health, even when we don't remember them. But some dreams are memorable. One of my patients, a stroke victim, complained to me some years ago that she was having very vivid dreams where she would look around and think 'This isn't happening, it's a dream', so she would then do her best to change it. I explained to her that she was describing lucid dreaming. Quite possibly, one reason for lucid dreaming in this case might be that since the stroke, the connections in her brain were finding new routes and trying to mend her. But this phenomenon provides opportunities.

I explained to my patient that just by thinking about walking or running, her nerves might trigger the muscles to respond. They might then move, in a very small way, so she might use her dreams to try to improve her mobility a little by teaching new nerve pathways to partly compensate for the damaged ones. After a stroke part of the brain has died, but new areas of the brain can to be used to bypass the damaged area, so new nerve pathways have to develop. This is a very slow and usually incomplete process, but in this case her dreaming about the movements she wanted to regain, had the potential to help her. This method of thinking about moving to improve ability has been used in some novel ways. I talked with a coach for the British Archery team and was told that some years ago they used a method of visualisation to improve their shots.

Not everyone can manage self-hypnosis, so instead the archers sat awake but relaxed. They sat with their eyes shut, without movement, but imagined that they were loosing an arrow that was a perfect shot. At the same time they were wired up to machinery that measured any nerve impulses in the muscles and it was discovered that exactly the same muscle activity sequence occurred as would be used during an actual shot, but minutely. So without actually practicing a single shot the archers were improving on their reflexes and honing their skills.

So what is a lucid dream exactly? In simple terms it is a dream where you are aware that you are dreaming and where you can alter the outcome.

While I was thinking about this section I had a dream where I was gardening and I stopped and turned away to tell my husband, in the dream, about lucid dreaming. I said that for it to be a lucid dream you have to know that you are dreaming, and then told him that this was a dream. I then said that you have to be able to take control of the dream, just as I was doing by discussing it with him. So because I had been thinking about lucid dreaming I had a lucid dream where I was explaining what a lucid dream was.

When I first came across the concept of lucid dreaming in my thirties I was confused. I was told what it entailed and didn't understand, because as far as I knew the person was describing normal dreaming. I couldn't imagine someone dreaming and not being 'awake' and aware within the dream.

The probable reason for this was that when we were young children and had bad dreams my mother told us that they were our dreams and we were in control, so we could change them and make them better. To do that you have to know you are dreaming. As a consequence we steadily learnt to be aware when something was a dream and to be able to control what happened. My mother explained that it was like a story, but it was our story so we could do what we liked. She was teaching us to develop lucid dreaming long before we were of school age and the ability never left. So I had ever since thought of this as normal dreaming.

In a study of lucid dreaming reported in New Scientist (12/6/10), Ursula Voss of the University of Frankfurt managed to record the brain waves of three volunteers during lucid dreaming which indicated a different brain activity from both wakefulness and normal sleep. Michael Crisch of the Max Planck Institute of Psychiatry in Munich, Germany used a high resolution MRI scan to investigate the brain activity of the lucid dreamers to see what was happening. This appeared to show highly coordinated activity in the frontal, parietal and temporal regions of the brain during lucidity. The dorso-lateral prefrontal cortex (DLPFC) was particularly active and thought to be important in higher states of consciousness. In other words they could see certain areas of the brain had become active that are not usually active during sleep or whilst awake. The same can be said of meditation; research into meditation also shows unusual brain activity.

It is thought that the greater coordination between these different areas of the brain might account for the awareness within lucid dreams, because analytical thought would be present as well as the sensory and emotional perception of normal dream state. There was a slower brain activity (40 hertz) that was similar to the waking state. This means that the person seemed to be in a slightly awake state whilst also asleep and dreaming.

The researchers hoped that the study might help people with mental illness, those who are unable to distinguish between imagination and reality, even when they are awake, as with schizophrenia; which is the opposite experience to lucidity.

In other tests with lucid dreamers by Robert Piller of Pomona College in Claremont, California, it was found that tasks such as reading, writing and speaking were extremely hard to perform in a dream whereas painting, drawing or humming a tune within the dream were easier. This is thought to be because the right hemisphere, the creative side is more active during sleep, whereas the left, language side is relatively inactive.

So how do you find out if you are already a lucid dreamer, or encourage this state of altered consciousness if you are not? Apparently the people most likely to dream lucidly are those who concentrate single-mindedly on a task during the day, which suggests a degree of obsession or perseverance in the personality. Then, while you are dreaming you need to ask yourself if you are awake or asleep. If you practise this during the day while you are awake it has been found to be is easier to do in your sleep.

Plan your dream before you go to sleep and when you wake up recall as many dreams as you can. And lastly, it works best if you have woken and then gone back to sleep again. If you find yourself in a dream and are aware that it is a dream and can change what is happening at will then you are there, you are experiencing a lucid dream.

There are things you can do in a dream to see if you are dreaming. Curiously if you jump off a chair you seem to reach the floor too slowly, or if you switch a light on it doesn't work. This suggests that the unconscious cannot keep up with sudden changes.

Because people who have lucid dreams are better able to control their thoughts whilst dreaming, they may have better access to their unconscious minds. This means that they might also have better access to past life memories. As well as this perhaps they would be less easily diverted under hypnosis and better able to recall real events rather than slipping into imagination. Perhaps then lucid dreamers would make the best subjects for regression hypnosis and be better able to stay on track.

Children who report the most dreams appear to be those with better developed mental imagery in their waking lives. This is not necessarily a better imagination, just a more visual way of thinking. Dreaming is thought to be associated with the development of the parietal lobes of the brain which are linked to visual-spatial abilities. So it's about shapes and spaces; this harks back to the memories related to maps and finding your way around that was mentioned earlier.

Curiously these visual-spatial abilities are most highly developed in dyslexic people; albeit at the expense of word construction and or recognition. It would be entirely reasonable therefore to expect dyslexic people to dream more vividly than others.

I could find no study exploring this possibility; however, there are studies into dyslexia that demonstrate the enhanced visual-spatial ability. A 1996 survey of students at Central Saint Martins College of Art found that most of the art students were dyslexic and gained very high scores in visual-spatial tests. Indeed a degree of dyslexia could be a prerequisite to become an artist.

In 1984, Professor Norman Gechwind, then head of Harvard University neurology department, studied children gifted in creative subjects, who were also dyslexic. He believed that high levels of testosterone in late foetal development led to right hemisphere dominance in the brain and therefore led to better visual-spatial reasoning and creativity. Dyslexia is more about what a person can do than what they cannot.

There are high levels of lateral thinking and three dimensional problem solving abilities amongst dyslexic people. This leads to mechanical, technical as well as artistic and architectural abilities. In other words dyslexia is where the brain works better in some ways at the cost of abilities in other skills. Much as a really good physicist may have exceptional ability in abstract scientific thought but might lack the physical dexterity of a footballer. Nature has made humans into specialists who need to live in communities. In order to do this we need to get the best selection of abilities shared out amongst the individuals in the group. Specialised abilities are an asset to society not a disability.

The most common past life dream appears to be related to the memory of dying. Otherwise past life recall tends to be like normal daytime memories. This might be because the memory of the death itself may be suppressed during waking hours but insinuates itself into dream time. So practising lucid dreaming may be a useful avenue for adults hoping to remember their previous lives or to gain more detail.

Lucid dreaming, and indeed all of the skills found under the heading of altered consciousness, may also be completely natural specialisations. Many people are specialists, in that their skills are unbalanced so that they may have one thing they are good at. It's rare to find someone who is equally good at everything, or indeed equally poor at everything. So if you are unable to achieve lucid dreaming then it might not be in your particular skill repertoire. This should not be seen as a loss or failure; you probably have other different skills. Though oddly, most people don't value or recognise their own skills but seem to want skills that other people possess.

I think that for society to work at its best we should strive towards finding out what we ourselves can do best, rather than spending too much time worrying about things that other people can do or thinking that there are things we cannot do. We evolved to be different because difference and specialisation work for society to function properly. Difference should be something we can embrace.

This I find particularly pertinent, being on the autistic spectrum. High functioning autism is known to be a province of specialisation, in that we have a few enhanced skills, for example the ability to concentrate on one topic for a lifetime and focus on the facts. These varieties in humanity must have been selected for in evolution because they have an advantage, if not for the individual then for society as a whole. The differences in personality are probably to do with survival of the species. I keep McLeay's spectre stick insects. I started with three of these large insects and noticed that one hid down low under a leaf, one fed on more variety of leaves in a mid area of the cage and one was always at the top marching about and eating the best leaves. These are three different survival tactics. Personality exists even in insects, so of course we find perfectly valid differences in people too.

Sadly there are no shortcuts to higher states of consciousness. I have repeatedly told people that recreational drugs do not open the mind and are not a shortcut to enlightenment. Reported tests on psilocybin, the active ingredient of magic mushrooms, appear to confirm this. Robin Carhart-Harris at the Imperial College London injected 30 volunteers with psilocybin and scanned their brains and measured blood flow and connectivity. What he found was reduced blood flow and reduced connectivity. It would appear that rather than opening the mind, the effect was to shut the mind down and make it less connected. A brief outline of some of the later conclusions may be found in the following link. (http://beckleyfoundation.org/2017/07/26/what-is-the-ego-and-how-do-psychedelics-shut-it-down/)

When I had an electroencephalograph measuring my brain activity whilst using the paranormal ability of psychometry, the effect was quite the opposite. There was marked increase in activity and connections in several areas of the brain. I think it is reasonable to assume that drugs are not anything to do with any kind of higher consciousness, but perhaps fool people into thinking that the experience is something it's not. By limiting their brain function it's possible that the person has to fill in the missing connections using imagination, which would explain some of the effects.

Instead we might try to become more aware of everything and everyone around us. Connect rather than isolate ourselves, seek activity rather than opting out and probably most importantly, enjoy our differences.

Chapter 8

Connectivity

When my uncle Grahame died at the grand age of 91, nobody told me; which was a bit upsetting. Grahame was a lovely man; he had Tourette's, OCD and was almost certainly on the autistic spectrum, but nobody took any notice of the twitches, throat clearing or odd behaviour. He used to cut all of the irritating labels out of his clothing and tucked all of his clothing in, which gave him an eccentric countryman look. His house was clean but cluttered on every surface with collections of ornaments and knickknacks, every window sill, table top and shelf; overflowing display cabinets surrounded the walls. His mind was just as full and interesting as his home.

We had many similarities in temperament and when I was young he used to take me on long country walks with my older brother, or take us rowing on the river where we would look out for water voles and herons. In his later years we enjoyed e-mailing and exchanging philosophical ideas.

When Grahame was a bit slow replying to one of my e-mails I wondered if he was unwell. Once his reply became late enough to cause concern I tracked down one of the carers he liked and talked about and she told me that I'd missed the funeral. With a bit of research I managed to find out who was dealing with probate and the solicitor's details.

When I got in touch with the executor she seemed preoccupied with thinking that I wanted my uncle's money and oddly unaware that we had met on several occasions. Actually all I wanted was to find out why nobody told me and to ask if I could buy a couple of paintings from his estate. One was of a Welsh hillside I had painted for my uncle and aunt many years earlier and the other was the picture that hung in my grandmother's house for many years and represented part of my childhood. I was told that they had already been sold. Then I thought about the family photographs but was told that she hadn't found any.

Grahame had retired to Cornwall, where the family had originated from. As I lived many miles away in the middle of the country, visiting the solicitor to sort anything out was a problem. Fortunately however, my uncle had written to me when his wife was still alive saying that I should have the family photographs, since I was the only person likely to be interested in family history; both he and his wife had signed the letter. So I sent a copy of the letter to the solicitor and the family photographs appeared virtually by return post.

Because we had so nearly lost part of our history I ensured that every member of the family had copies of all of the pictures, which included formal photographs of relatives born in the 1800s. Then it occurred to me that here was an opportunity to write and research to discover more about the people in the photographs, many of whom I hadn't had the chance to meet. This too I could share with everyone in the family.

So I became engrossed in a family tree that grew extensively in an online site. It helped; not only was I grieving over the loss of my uncle, but the unusual circumstances had triggered a difficult reaction that caused me to grieve, at last, over the loss of my father and then, over the next few months, for everyone I had lost. So I continued to work hard on the family tree because work is often the best way to cope with out of control emotions; particularly grief.

The family tree grew sideways to encompass distant cousins and it went back; and I couldn't stop, I couldn't leave it alone. Once I had found all I could for my father's side, back to Cornwall in the 1500s, then sideways to distant cousins in Canada, Australia and New Zealand, I decided to expanded my mother's side and it discovered that it went back a very long way.

A number of my mother's family lines went back through landowners to Lords then many more lines diverged, then some started to converge again. Many lines passed through the Plantagenet Kings; others eventually went through the Vikings and the Kings and nobility of the whole of Europe and further afield. And it still kept going back. I finally decided to stop looking any further back than the year 800 and by then had several hundred lines, more than 60 of which went directly back to the Emperor Charlemagne.

Now, anyone who can add up will know that this becomes an absurdity. There were so few people living in the world over a thousand years ago that everybody is related. The world population has grown something like 35 times over since the year 800. So anyone with European ancestry will be related to Charlemagne and everybody will go back to kings somewhere along the way. When you look back 35 to 40 generations the number of descendants runs into many millions. We are all connected, we are all cousins.

Of course if you go back far enough you could find someone whom everyone on the planet is related to. Every human alive today does share a common ancestor, believed to be an African woman who lived around 200,000 years ago. This was discovered because all women inherit mitochondrial DNA from their mothers, so it can be traced back to show that we are all related to this one woman and are therefore all related to each other. We are truly one people; we are all connected by DNA.

We are of course all connected from the very start of life. All life on this planet developed from the same original simple celled organisms. We know this because we share DNA strands with all other living things including plants. Life over the whole planet can be looked upon as interconnected parts of the same energy; one life. The variety of plants and animals only occurs because sometimes an individual changes a bit, so that it is slightly different from its parents. Only these minor changes and a great deal of time, separates living things from each other.

This is probably true of life on other planets too. It's an interesting thought that we are liable to have more DNA in common with slugs or lichen than we would with extraterrestrial life forms. So there is no chance of cross-breeding with life forms away from this planet. Indeed, scientific thought suggests that ET is most likely to be some sort of intelligent octopus rather than a hominid. Mammals only dominated on this planet due to a series of fluke changes and mass extinctions.

So we are all connected. It's a New Age phrase but it happens to be right on so many levels. On the macrocosm, all energy and matter were one at the start of the universe. Perhaps when everything burst into existence and atoms were created, the energy that would eventually create life was fragmented into countless billions of units along with matter. Perhaps consciousness itself existed in potential form. Matter is recycled; atoms were created in early super suns and the same matter makes up everything, including us. It seems logical then that the energy that makes life would also be recycled. But once, maybe only for a moment, it was a single something along with everything else in the universe.

Maybe at the end of this universe everything will coalesce into one as the universe collapses before it starts up once again in a new big bang. Some scientists now believe that the whole universe is eternally recycled, reincarnated, collapsing into a singularity and bursting forth all over again. One of the hypotheses relating to recycling of the universe can be found via this link. (https://www.space.com/2372-recycled-universe-theory-solve-cosmic-mystery.html)

Physical life wants to exist. In experiments recreating the conditions where life is thought to have started the units that make up the building blocks for biological compounds are drawn together with some ease, given that the environment is conducive. (https://www.wired.com/2009/05/ribonucleotides/)

We might get a glimpse into a sense of the connectedness of all things quite unexpectedly. I had an experience which was hard to quantify but is not completely unusual. As a teenager, whilst walking home one afternoon from a family friend's house, the sunlight was flickering through the trees creating a strobe-like effect. Momentarily mesmerised by this I suddenly became aware of the life within the trees, their energy and presence. Then this slightly out-of-body sensation expanded exponentially and I felt part of the ebb and flow of all life. I felt the energy within plants and animals and their births and deaths in a continuous cycle. I wasn't thinking that life was connected, I was feeling it intensely and it was totally outside my control. It only lasted a few minutes, but was an astounding experience.

It was more than forty years later before I realised that this was recognised as a mystical experience, being at one with everything. The Australian Institute of Parapsychological Research listed it as an external, extroversive experience in a subgroup of 'merging with nature'. The phenomena had been thoroughly researched and this particular type of occurrence was recorded it as happening to two percent of the people researched who had admitted to some kind of mystical experience. (http://www.aiprinc.org/mystical/)

It's apparently typical that most mystical experiences come suddenly, unexpectedly and only last a few minutes. Less intense experiences plateaux and last longer. Triggers can be internal or external; relaxation and rhythmic influences are listed in the research. There is often an alteration in the person after such an experience.

Religious leaders, scientist, philosophers and writers appear notable amongst those who are lucky enough to enjoy these life changing experiences, but it is not exclusive, many people have these. I wonder if the episode itself is a precursor to the route a person's life might take later, as it is also indicated as being life enhancing and motivational. In other words the experience might be the reason itself for later success.

But the one outstanding feature is that after such an experience, there is never a doubt that all life is connected; that we are just a part of an intricate web of life and dependent on this support network.

Sadly this sense of connectedness seems a bit lost to us. We are all distant cousins but seem determined to fall out and war with each other, often over small things such as a difference of opinion, forgetting that we are meant to be different because we are not identical clones.

Indeed, it is important to be aware of our individual personalities. There is a psychological condition where people have a fuzzy edge between where they end and the next person begins. This occurs in societies or families where everybody is forced to be the same and behave the same way. It is very important that children learn, by the age of two at the latest, that they are separate individuals and allowed to have their own ideas. Without that you end up with societies that are so intolerant of the slightest difference that they see outsiders as non-people and therefore targets for annihilation.

This paranoia in a society is described as one step above insanity and one below dictatorship and explains some of the most intolerant and violent social groups. The simplest description of this can be found in 'Families and How to Survive Them' by John Cleese and Robin Skinner under sections relating to fuzzy boundaries. An easy discussion of this idea can be found in this link (https://www.psychologytoday.com/blog/prescriptions-life/201301/boundaries-its-time-say-no-when-you-need)

When we remember our previous lives we have a strong desire to reconnect. It's the main driving force when trying to track down who we were. We want to go back and see everyone again, to know what happened next, to make a connection, to breach the gap in time. Yet we have probably lived lives with everyone else. We could make that connection anywhere and everywhere.

Although we are connected and related to each other, there are times when we all feel isolated or disconnected. This might have nothing to do with our personal circumstances, but can be from within. For some people it is a transitory state, for others a more deep-seated sense of separation prevails. But the awareness itself can compound and intensify the experience. Everybody knows how it is possible to be surrounded by people yet feel utterly alone, if only for a short time.

To avoid this feeling we all seek to connect with the world around us in the things we do. From earliest childhood the importance of interaction with others and with our surroundings is paramount, essential to our healthy development. Certainly babies constantly seek to connect, often making it very clear that they need someone all of the time and not just to care for their immediate survival requirements. We all need other people at least some of the time.

Communication means different things to different people but the end goal is the same; to connect, to understand another person, to feel less alone, to be understood.

This may mean joining in with the light-hearted banter to be accepted as one of a group, or it could involve achieving a profound eureka moment in intense conversation with a close friend. Or it could be about working together on a project for work or just for the pleasure of it.

Sadly it may also mean joining in with a destructive group of people just to fulfil the primal need for a sense of tribal belonging. Sometimes it just means taking on a group identity, which can be as harmless as adopting a certain way of dressing or joining in with a particular music style. Or it could be as destructive as identifying with a dangerous political movement. We all need to feel we fit in somewhere.

Through sport we compete with others and echo the prestige of the hunt that our ancient ancestors competed in for survival. But also, ultimately, we compete with ourselves and the physical world around us. Through our efforts we can achieve a sense of euphoria, but it is our physical relationship with the world and our connection to it that translates the interaction. Our bodies were built for effort and rejoice in competition.

Work is usually more than just a means to an income. We need to feel part of the work community, to be involved. Appreciation is just another form of feeling connected to others, to be part of something more that just ourselves. We will try to do our job well and take pride in what we do because we understand that we are connected and that what we do affects others and therefore affects us. If that sense of being part of the team is absent it can lead to feelings of inadequacy, disconnection and dissatisfaction.

We tend to think of verbal and written communication as being the way we connect, but it is not the only way. Normally, verbal communication is not even how we are first drawn to people we like. We have a way of communicating of which we are hardly even aware.

There is an exercise used to train psychologists in 'family therapy' which shows that people who have had similar experiences or who hold similar values are drawn to each other, without the need for any conversation at all. It is an instinct, our outlook shows on our faces.

In 'Families and how to survive them' by Robin Skynner and John Cleese (Methuen 1983) such a training course is described. People had to pair up and then make groups of four, without talking to each other, but by choosing someone with whom they felt instinctively comfortable or who might fit into their own family.

When the groups of four sat down and talked they discovered that they had many things in common, like absent fathers. In one exercise discussed, the last group to get together, the wallflowers, thought that they would have nothing in common because they were just the ones left over at the end, but in fact they had all been fostered or adopted and felt rejected in early life.

It is this instinct that I referred to in a previous chapter when discussing how we choose to return to a new life. I feel that the same instinct that draws us to like-minded people also draws us to the people we will be reborn to. I have no memory of conscious planning.

So apparently we connect with each other in unconscious ways. Psychology recognises that we have this deeper core connection of which we are virtually unaware. But our connections may go further.

The psychologist Carl Jung talked about the collective unconscious as experience derived from the whole of humanity. In other words an inherited part of the mind that we have in common that may be instinct based.

But I feel that this term can be interpreted further to mean a collective mind we can share with each other without being aware, to be connected as a group mind at a deeper level. This is a little similar to a view called monopsychism, a belief where all people are thought to share a common consciousness, soul, mind or intellect, and which appears in slightly varying forms as a part of the belief systems of Jewish Kabala, of the 12th century philosophy of Averroism and of Rastafarian beliefs. Some Mystical Judeo-Christian-Islamic beliefs also hold that we all derive from the one soul of Adam and are connected in that way.

The conscious mind is the tiny part of ourselves that we are aware of most of the time, but it is just the tip of the iceberg. The unconscious we reach through dreams or access to retrieve knowledge or memories, often without knowing how we knew those things. Like answering a question in a quiz by some instinct, then being surprised that we were right. The collective unconscious might be seen as a third part of the mind, a part we have in common, our inherited instinct, or perhaps the shared mind. A much larger part of us that we are barely aware is there. Looking at it this way, events in our lives that seem coincidental might only happen because we are connected to each other and affect each other.

Taking this sharing of the mind to be an actual connection, rather than just something we inherit in common, you might imagine an unconscious connection reaching out between us like a web. You might be able to envisage something akin to a single organism. One creature called humanity. Or take it a stage further still and see the whole of life as one complex interconnected super-consciousness, or rather a super-unconsciousness, of every living thing on this planet. In this way we could be interacting unconsciously with overall goals, for example the survival of as much life as possible.

Carl Jung was interested in coincidence, or what he called synchronicity. During a heated discussion with Freud, Jung told him of a dream he had of a bookcase falling. Moments later a bookcase fell against Freud. There are many ways of looking at synchronicity; but both synchronicity and the collective unconscious are probably interrelated.

When I searched for my past life family in Ireland I was lucky that the ruins of my old home were still standing. Yet they were not there for much longer, making way for a housing estate. I was lucky that the brothers had managed to find each other again only a couple of years earlier. I was even lucky that the trail of the many helping me just happened to be there at the right time. These events were synchronic.

Our connectivity can be seen in many ways, like an experience that contains unusual synchronicity. However, we need to be cautious about coincidence. Often it is just an unusual juxtaposition of events and has no relevance. A reincarnation case should never rely on coincidence; evidence is vital.

But if we are all connected through a collective unconscious, our striving for knowledge and understanding is probably much more of a joint effort than we are aware. Perhaps I was just one of many people directed in my search by everyone else. I needed to find my past life family, maybe the unconscious-all-of-us needed to help me, or at least help someone, to find a past life family too. Perhaps in order to answer a few questions that quite a few of us had.

So the events that happened at the right time could have been an unconscious connection. Perhaps I was just a tool of the larger organism of humanity along with everyone else who finds the answers we all need. If we take the example of scientific research, every researcher who gets a lucky break might be helped by all of the rest of us, not only because parallel research leads scientists along the same paths, but also we may be led unconsciously. To be in the right place at the right time, to meet the right people who can help, to see the one thing that helps get the breakthrough needed; this may be one function of our connectedness. Along with the huge amount of work required for any scientific advance, there is often a lot of apparent luck involved. My thought is that this might not be luck but unconscious direction.

One way of looking at our connectedness might be to think of us all linked in much the same way as our computers are connected to the Internet. Each computer is individual but via the Internet has connection to all others. The collective unconscious could be a connection between us at such a deep level that we are usually completely unaware. A different kind of connection might help us understand precognition, where the link is across time.

I almost never read newspapers; I prefer to listen to the news on the radio, if I bother at all. Television news is so visual that it is often disturbing and news generally is depressing and there is nothing I can do to make things better, so I avoid it. So I have often wondered why it was that I happened to read the one newspaper that reported the invention of a prototype laser microscope that I had predicted several years earlier.

The description of the laser microscope was included in 'Past Lives Future Lives' and first 'seen' under hypnosis in 1993. I described it as a prominent instrument used in the future, in alarmingly accurate detail. Then on 21st February 1996 I picked up a copy of the Daily Telegraph someone had left at a café. The book was already being printed by then, so the confirmation of this prediction appeared in the next book, 'Journeys Through Time'.

The laser microscope I had described as being capable of looking at living tissue. Some of my description was almost word for word what the article said three years later.

So how does precognition work? I am sure everyone who experiences precognition from time to time must have wondered the same thing. We have no definitive evidence about how precognition might work yet, but the way it seems to happen could give us a bit of insight into what might be going on.

Seeing this invention a few years in advance of its development was no doubt a really useful and accurate premonition, but just happening to read the one newspaper with an article about it on exactly the right day might seem like an amazing coincidence; unless we are looking at the events in the wrong order.

So was I guided to the right newspaper on the right day and taken to the exact page, so that I would read the article and find confirmation of the specific precognitive experience I'd had several years earlier? This sounds a bit far fetched, an amazing synchronicity, and is one reason why I have wondered if the connection is slightly different.

It makes more sense if the events are turned around; perhaps the newspaper came first. Not in chronological order, clearly, but the events could still have occurred back to front, if we could just get past the little problem of their being stuck in times that were separated by a few years in the wrong order.

First, let's look at why I was reading a newspaper. I was on holiday, so it was one of the few times when I might be sitting in a café and finding a newspaper lying about waiting to be read. It was the newspaper that my mother read, so I knew it had a science section; I wasn't interested in the news. I went directly to the science section and read an article about a laser microscope and read about its capabilities; that it was used for looking at living tissue. So far there was nothing strange in this.

Now what if, at this point, while I was reading the article, the details of the information were relayed back to an earlier version of me, in a connection across time. This way at the same time as reading about the microscope I simultaneously already knew about it in the past.

So it was a precognitive experience because I could remember the article whilst reading it for the first time, but more importantly I had already published details about it in a book, details that were as specific as the article but importantly, no more specific. In fact, although they were not quite as complete they were eerily similar. It looked as though what I had spoken about and written about was the newspaper article itself rather than just the invention; albeit several years before the newspaper was printed and before the laser microscope was invented.

If it is looked at this way around it is no longer an astounding coincidence that I picked up the right newspaper and looked at the exact page on the exact date that the article appeared, or that what I said several years beforehand was so similar to the newspaper article. Because this event may have come first; if the newspaper came first it could have been relayed back in time as I was reading it so of course the detail would be the same as the article.

This is only one explanation for how premonition might work; it has its flaws, in that as far as we know time travel is not possible; but time travel for thoughts? When time travel is discussed the thinking is usually about moving something physical. But the possibility of just thought travelling through time seems to have been neglected. The physics would be very different for matter or the energy of thought, which one assumes might be electrical.

Physical time travel would require faster than light speed travel. The problem is that nothing can travel faster than light, except perhaps a post big bang universe going through inflation. So physical time travel has pretty much been ruled out.

One view of time travel is to envisage two points in time that make contact with each other; so that time might loop back on itself. Again, physical travel would probably not work but thought? It would only need a brief moment for the contents of the article to be sent as a thought. This would work as an answer for all reported precognitive experiences. These events only tend to last a very short period of time, usually a few seconds.

It is difficult to find a logical explanation for precognition but it works so there has to be an answer. It exists and needs to be studied and explained; not explained away or dismissed. It is possible that the science already exists to study the phenomenon but I would not claim to have sufficient knowledge to be able to find it for myself. There is a huge body of work on precognition, mainly to demonstrate that it exists rather than to find the cause. Yet the 'how' is so much more interesting than the 'if'.

Another precognitive experience was also fulfilled, some eighteen years after I talked about it under hypnosis during the 1990 sessions. I'd described bill boards in shopping centres that move like a loop of film.

Indeed this is now exactly what happens. The first one I saw was in Milton Keynes and was an advertisement for a Johnny English film with Rowan Atkinson. The first film came out in 2003 but I think the bill board was later. Either way it was a long time after my description. In the bill board Johnny English was standing then moved to look at his watch.

At a deeply unconscious level we are all connected; which is why one way of understanding both precognition and telepathy (thought sharing) is by looking at the ways we are all connected with each other. We may also be connected to those who are between lives.

As a child I was able to see and talk with two World War Two soldiers, who were real people to me whom I couldn't see all of the time. I was told that they were imaginary friends, even though I lack imagination. Many years later I discovered that people are said to have spirit guides and wondered if these friends were guides. There are two schools of thought. One that we have real people who are in spirit and who help us in subtle ways through our lives; the other, that they are unconscious archetypes from our inner mind that we draw on to help us make decisions.

On odd occasions I have been aware of unseen people around me. When asked if they are real or just archetypes of the subconscious mind I have to say that my slightly sceptical and analytical side would like to dismiss the possibility of their being real, but every few years something else happens to reinforce the experiences.

As a child I was certain that they were real people who had been soldiers; they were too flawed and complex to be thought of any other way. So overall I am willing to see this as a connection to the other side of our existence. I have also come across mediums who explained that they were able to see spirits as children, but then just sense them as they grow up but no longer see them.

In 'Memories of Heaven' by Dr Wayne W Dyer and Dee Garnes, there is a collection of anecdotes about children who remember past lives or between lives. But it also has a section about children who see spirits which is titled 'Invisible Friends and Spiritual Visitations'. Whilst reading it I was reminded of the two soldiers in my childhood. I had always wondered who they were. I thought they had known each other but wondered why they came and talked to me, especially the slightly older one who seemed interested in my welfare.

After finding out more about Charles Savage's father, who died in December 1942 in uniform, in Egypt, I began to wonder if it was he who watched over me.

There is also a great deal of evidence that we can connect with loved ones who have died. Most people talk to their relatives and many sense their presence. Driving back from the nursing home after my father died I was suddenly aware of his voice saying "That was odd; it was all whoosh and vroom," describing the suddenness of leaving the body in his typical onomatopoeic way.

Because of this connectedness it might be said that in many ways we can never be alone, even though we might feel lonely.

I have described here how I interpret the collective unconscious; as a larger mind, humanity, and maybe all of life, as one, all connected; but a connection that we are only able to access in very unconscious ways. Any organism has needs, and finding answers to things we want to understand, for whatever reason, might be one of those needs. The larger mind could delegate parts of the problem to its smaller units. We the individuals would be those smaller units. But we see ourselves as separate beings and our achievements as personal. Yet we know even at a conscious level that very few of our achievements are completely ours alone and we all rely on help at some point.

I doubt we are as separate as we think. Even if we ignore the possibility of an unconscious connection we still need each other; we are linked and reliant on each other. But I think we are connected at the deepest spiritual level.

A jigsaw is made up of many differently shaped pieces and only when they all fit together do we have a picture. We too are all different, but all are needed to make the picture complete.

Chapter 9

What Are We?

If we look in the mirror what we see in our reflection is mostly a dead layer of cells on the outer part of our skin. But we live in this skin. Our physical bodies are made from elements that are as old as the stars. These have been recycled over and over and used to make many different things since they came into existence and have eventually been used to build our bodies.
So if everything is made of the stuff of stars what about souls?
If our life energy is recycled through reincarnation then it would have to have been there from the very start, in just the same way as the elements that make our bodies were formed at the start.
This means that whatever energy makes up the soul it must also have been a part of life when life first began; and life began very small. It's difficult to try to think of the kind of soul that might inhabit very simple organisms, but whatever it is, this spark of life must have always been in everything alive.
This is at last something that science is starting to discuss; looking at the brain as being similar to a biological computer and the soul as a programme. The article here also suggests, as I am, that souls may have existed since the beginning of time. American physicist Dr Stuart Hameroff and mathematical physicist Sir Roger Penrose both argue that the soul is maintained in micro tubules of brain cells and is released to the universe after death. (http://irelease.org/scientists-found-that-the-soul-doesnt-die-it-goes-back-to-the-universe/)
Looking at the kind of soul that might have been here at the beginning is difficult. Perhaps it's easier to think about the souls of individuals who are self-aware; from the point when life reached consciousness, but when was that? People tend to think that only humans have a level of consciousness that includes self awareness, but many animals demonstrate awareness of themselves as distinct from others.
Indeed science now seems set to accept the self awareness of higher animals to the point where long overdue legislation may

soon protect these species from abuse. Discussions are under way to give rights to higher animals for their protection.

In July 2012 a group of scientists attended the first annual Francis Crick Memorial Conference. Francis Crick was one of the researchers who discovered DNA and studied consciousness. The result of the meeting was the Cambridge Declaration on Consciousness, put forward by the neuroscientists David Edelman, Philip Low and Christof Koch. Part of this declaration states "non-human animals have the neuroanatomical, neurochemical and neurophysiological substrates of conscious states along with the capacity to exhibit intentional behaviours". (https://www.newscientist.com/article/mg21528836-200-animals-are-conscious-and-should-be-treated-as-such/)

What kind of awareness do other animals have? Chimpanzees taught to communicate with sign language talk about their own possessions and distinguish between what is theirs and what is not. They identify themselves and others with personal names. They are most definitely self aware.

Elephants in Thailand have been taught to paint and now, as well as painting very attractive, complex and regular patterns, will happily paint flowers, trees and even elephants. The paintings elephants make of elephants are often reminiscent of early cave paintings and are as precise and detailed, simple line drawings, demonstrating a very high degree of self awareness. Elephants in the wild are amongst the very few animals that will adopt orphaned young, showing a consideration of others who are not their direct responsibility and therefore outside of simple instinct.

Dolphins appear to have distinct sounds indicating a different name for each separate member of their herd. Marine researchers now talk about communicating with dolphins within a few years.

Many animals mourn the death of one of their family. When a chimp named Pansy lay dying at Blair Drummond Safari Adventure Park in Stirling in 2008, her companions stroked her and comforted her. When she died the other chimps checked her mouth to confirm that she was dead and one chimp, Chippy, tried to revive her, twice, by beating on her chest. This sparked an interest in the way animals other than humans perceive death. Wild chimps have been observed to stay with dead troop members and becoming upset at the loss. It has long been known that elephants spend time with the bones of dead elephants and dolphins swim alongside corpses for long periods. (New Scientist 20/10/12)

All of these things suggest minds capable of seeing themselves as individuals and identifying with and caring about others. These are indications of minds that are self aware and as a consequence perhaps, souls that are evolved too.

Many animals use tools. Birds of a number of species use sticks to poke out food and in laboratory experiments can work out how to use stones to raise the water level in a tube to access food. Sea otters use a stone on their chest to strike shellfish against to break them open and thrushes use a stone 'anvil' to crush snail shells.

But this may go further, a chimp has been observed making tools, rather than just using them. This is a step forwards and suggests that if we did do something silly to ourselves and we all died out, there may be another hominid evolving that could eventually take our place. (http://www.bbc.co.uk/earth/story/20150818-chimps-living-in-the-stone-age)

This is rather reminiscent of the film 'Planet of the Apes' perhaps, but quite a reasonable assumption. Nature will always try to fill any evolutionary void. If we were not here, in time other species would fill the gap. I wonder if the souls of the extinct species would return to a similar place in a rising species; if we managed to cause our own demise would we still come back as another animal; quite probably.

A study into memory looking at the hippocampus (part of the brain processing memories) of rats, suggests they think their way through a maze they have already been through and may imagine future paths they could take. Constructive imagination or problem solving is a sign of consciousness. A chimp at Furuvik zoo in Sweden gathers rocks and hides them so he can use them as missiles to throw at visitors later. These are examples of thinking ahead and planning suggestive of consciousness and higher thought processes.

Insects in experiments can tell if a food pile has five items or six items, and will go for the larger pile, but this just shows that they can count, not that they are self aware.

In the end it would be very difficult to pin down awareness or higher thought, so it should probably remain at some point in the long distant past when higher animals as well as our own ancestors, developed co-operation between individuals and consideration for each other, as happens, for example, in a wolf pack.

So we are self aware co-operative individuals; but that is only a tiny part of the story. This might glimpse at the part of us that relates to our socialisation, but there are many other things affecting our physicality and behaviour that do not appear at all human, but are still part of us.

We think of ourselves being entirely human, but much of our genetic material is not even mammalian. Some years ago it was reported that almost half of our DNA is derived from viruses (New Scientist 30/1/10). Many of the viruses that attack us just cause illness and then move on, like 'flu, or a cold, but some viruses never leave their hosts. Virulent retroviruses may kill, but survivors can co-evolve. Both the host and the virus begin to live together in co-operation, both slightly changed but forever linked together. This has happened again and again to every animal alive today.

(http://www.pbs.org/wgbh/nova/next/evolution/endogenous-retroviruses/)

This estimation has since been updated and it is now believed that we are almost wholly derived from viruses. The earliest life form, a single cell, then attacked by another primitive organism, a virus, eventually develops into a multi cell organism by the combination of both. Then the process repeats over and over to produce more complex organisms, but the additions are virus in origin.

It is thought that viruses evolved from plasmids, which are fragments of DNA in living cells. They may have escaped to exist independently from some of the earliest cells on earth by co-opting some of their hosts DNA to form a capsid shell (New Scientist 26 August 2017).

Our genome contains many thousands of retroviruses that have changed and become a part of us, to our mutual benefit. Each change causes development, and retroviruses may be part of the drive behind evolution. We are the survivors of countless viral attacks, but we are also part virus. So the question is, so whose body is it?

More and more it becomes possible to see our body as just the support system that we live in; our short-term home.

Part of our viral component seems to remain slightly adrift, acting only to turn other genes on or off. Jumping genes (some of the genetic material first identified as being derived from retroviruses) can move over gene sequences switching them on or off, making epigenetic changes, to alter our genetic data, including our ability to fight infection or our susceptibility to disease.

This can happen as a result of changes in our environment and is the fastest way we can evolve because it changes the individual and immediate generations. It was discovered that women who lived through some years of hunger, as many did during the war, tended to have smaller children, but then much taller grandsons. From a survival viewpoint this is probably to aid survival of the first generation during lean years, but then to produce stronger hunters to help feed the next generation.

Even where people share the same genes, changes can be made. A pair of identical twins had the gene that causes a much increased risk of breast cancer. One of them had the gene switched on, but it was found that the other had the gene switched off. So, one went for preventative surgery, whilst the other was deemed safe. ('Survival of the sickest'- Dr S Moalem)
Without the ever added viral components we would not be human. During early research into retrovirus incorporation essential genes derived from viruses were found to be

controlling embryo development and brain function and therefore an integral part of us.

We are also host to trillions of bacteria and other micro-organisms, outnumbering our own cells ten to one and called a microbiome. These are beneficial to us and many are essential to our health. There are bacteria in our guts that help us break down food to gain better nutrition, particularly from plant foods. We need their help; we probably couldn't survive without them.

But now there is a problem; antibiotics are destroying the friendly bacteria of our microbiome, sometimes permanently, and damaging our health long term. Bacteroides fragilis helps keep the immune system in balance. Without it we may be more liable to develop autoimmune diseases like Crohn's disease and multiple sclerosis. Both illnesses have a genetic component but bacteria may be the other part of the story. A loss of the bacterium Helicobacter pylori appears to be linked to weight gain. (Scientific American, June 2012).

Martin Blaser, a microbiologist at New York University found that low doses of antibiotic given to mice caused a reduction in the bacterium Lactobacillus, which is linked to lowering the risk of cancer. This suggests that antibiotic use can damage our ability to fight such disease. Indeed it was found that infection and our immune response to infection helps us fight cancer.

Babies given antibiotics during the first six months of life are more likely to be overweight by the age of seven, according to research by Teresa Ajslev and colleagues at Copenhagen University Hospital, Denmark (New Scientist 31/3/12). This is thought to be due to damage to our bacterial companions.

There is a natural and much safer alternative to the use of antibiotics; bacteriophage, a virus family that eats specific bacteria and do no harm to us, but we cannot currently use it. Drug companies are unlikely to put bacteriophage through testing and on to general use as it could affect sales of antibiotics and therefore profits. So although they are safe and can completely cure infections like MRSA they are unlikely to be used.

(https://www.ncbi.nlm.nih.gov/pmc/articles/PMC90351/)

Although most people think of their physical body as being one organism I have always thought of us as colonies. You may think you are one person, a whole living thing, but in some ways you are a collection of different smaller units coexisting to create one larger functioning living thing. In other words we are in charge of a body that is made up of many units connected and working together as one. Our collection of viruses and bacteria are part of this organism that we recognise as us; our body.

It also appears that many cells in our bodies seem to have a life of their own, functioning as though they are separate units that just happen to do something that aids the survival of the whole body- and therefore help maintain the environment in which they exist. Take blood cells; they are free to travel throughout our bodies and interact with other cells including invading bacteria or viruses. Some white blood cells spend their time hunting and 'eating' invading bacteria as though they were just living their own lives in an environment that happens to be the larger body that is us.

So I see each of us as collections of smaller biological units working as one fully functional individual. Then at the same time I see each of these complex units, us, as connected in a deep psychological way to all other living things; like one organism of life on the planet earth. Looking at it this way it becomes difficult to know what you are.

In the same way that the body may not be entirely one single organism, but a colony including viruses and bacteria, people can function as one mind made of many, not just as a collective unconscious as described in the previous chapter, but also in quite a different way, as a society.

This can be without much conscious awareness, each person working within the framework of society without necessarily considering the whole. And many people do live their lives without thinking much about how society works. However, it is relatively easy to picture how societies function, by looking from the workers up to companies and beyond, or to start at the top and look at governments and work down to the individuals. For everything to function properly this interdependent system has to balance. This is one of the ways we interact and rely on each other; in a physical sense as a society.

There is another complication to the picture of who we really are. And that is that we might not be in control of ourselves as much as we think we are. Our minds are not just that bit of us we think of as ourselves, it is much more complicated. Our conscious mind, the part we are aware of, is only the smallest part of who we really are; the rest is mostly hidden from us.

Neuro-psychologists describe our mind as containing a host of unconscious personalities that react to situations often before our conscious mind is aware of what is happening. Many sports cannot be competed in at a conscious level because, for example, a fast ball in cricket travels too fast for the conscious mind to follow. Yet cricketers can still hit a fast ball; they just do it before they consciously realise it has happened.

There are many daily events in which the same is true. In any learnt situation the learning process involves delegating part of the information to unconscious control, bit by bit. If we learn to do something complicated this is especially important.

Driving a car becomes partially unconscious as we learn. The mechanism of driving needs to be instinctive so that we can concentrate on the process of driving safely and looking at the road and our surroundings without having to think about how we change gear. An emergency stop can happen much faster than our awareness for the need to stop. We need the unconscious mind to act without us, and let us catch up afterwards, because otherwise we cannot respond quickly enough in an emergency.

If we have to take the time to think about what we are doing at a conscious level, it would not happen soon enough. Heroes jump into a situation to do what has to be done without any thought, because there is no time for thought, only unconscious action.

People can become annoyed with themselves; because some of the unconscious parts are in disagreement about a particular action.

We all do things without consciously thinking, and then sometimes become irritated by what we did. We respond on a primal, instinctive level and think that this is the real us, but it is only a part of us, and a very small part at that. We react to events and then have to catch up with ourselves.

It is probably impossible for us to be aware of all of our thought processes at one time because so much is going on without our knowing. But we can gain some insight into the greater working of our minds. Meditation, hypnosis and even sleep, allow us a small window into the vast unconscious.

Through sleep we can find out how we really feel about something and decide on the action we should take. Try it. Ask yourself a question before you go to sleep, writing it down so that you remember in the morning. When you wake up (check the written question if necessary) you will probably find that your thoughts on the issue are clearer. You tend to know what to do because while you were asleep the whole of your mind, the largest part of you, in its myriad of facets and archetypes, has been working on the problem for you.

Perhaps the real you is your unconscious and only reachable through sleep, meditation or hypnosis. Perhaps this gives us insight into who it is who changes bodies from life to life.

There are other ways that we may not be reacting to things fully as ourselves; our actions may be controlled by infections and parasites.

All animals are affected by parasites and infections. Many of these alter behaviour to suit their own needs. The most common parasite in people, outside of the tropics, is caught mainly from cats, soil or undercooked meat- Toxoplasmosis gondii. This occurs in the soil and is transferred to rats and then on to cats and often accidentally ends up in us. About a fifth of us in Britain carry the infection and up to two thirds in the rest of Europe -possibly due to the enjoyment of undercooked meats.

In rats it is in the interests of the parasite to alter the rat's behaviour to make them a little more reckless so that they may more easily be caught by a cat, so that the parasite can complete its life cycle. (J.P. Webster 'Rats, cats, people and parasites; the impact of latent toxoplasmosis on behaviour' microbes and infection, 2001)

In people, the first flush of infection is 'flu like symptoms, but in the latent stage cysts are laid down in the brain and may last a lifetime.

Studies show that people infected with T.gondii are 2.6% more likely to be involved in traffic accidents, have slower reactions in tests, seem more attracted to danger and tend to be prone to feelings of guilt. Infected men are more suspicious and jealous; women are friendlier, easy-going and more conscientious.

There has also been a link between T.gondii and schizophrenia. In one study children who grew up with cats were found to be 53% more likely to develop schizophrenia or bipolar disorder. This doesn't mean that T.gondii is the cause of schizophrenia (indeed cannabis is indicated as a trigger agent in at least one form of the disease, some say all). But it may have some action in creating the higher incidence; perhaps by changing mental states or brain chemistry. (S.F. Torrey and R.H. Yolken 'Toxoplasmosis and schizophrenia' –Emerging Infections Dis 2003)

However, schizophrenia does seem to act like an infection in that it appears suddenly in otherwise healthy people, usually around late teens to early adulthood. After the initial acute stage one third of people affected recover fully, another third recover but need medication, whilst a further third suffer lifelong problems despite medication. There are also epigenetic components (switching genes on or off) to schizophrenia and possibly genetic ones as well. Scientists seem a long way from being able to predict this complex disease.

Other infections may also change our behaviour. Streptococcus throat infections in childhood are believed to be associated with anxiety and obsessive compulsive disorder. On top of that any imbalance in hormone function can alter mood, perception and reactions.

So what are we? And how much control do we have anyway? Well after all of this the answer is probably that it doesn't matter. We function, we can alter our behaviour and try to be better people; we can work within society for the greater good.

We are partly our body, but this is also just where we live; we reside within it. We are partly our mind, however much it may be influenced by the chemistry of our hormones or even the bacteria that live with us. But this is not all we are.

The workings of the body and the brain might be fascinating from a biological point of view but we are more than this. For our soul, it doesn't matter if our body is made up of other organisms that have co-evolved to function as one. It doesn't matter that we are part virus and dependent on bacteria for our survival. It doesn't matter if our behaviour is subtly altered by infections, disease and our own chemistry; we are not just the body, it is not the whole of us. Our body is a vessel, and though it is important that we keep it in good order so that we are better able to function, it is not everything. We are the soul within the body.

So the idea of changing bodies, from one life to another, should not be a concern. Even the fittest and best looked after body gets old and wears out eventually, but we don't. An overhaul and reassessment, a bit of a rest, and we are ready to give it another go. We are the soul that is transplanted into a brand new tiny body with the responsibility to get it right, or at least to try.

The thing that matters far more than the body we have, is how we live our lives. We are reliant on the care and consideration of others for our own survival and it is essential that we offer the best we can in return. We live in societies, not as isolated individuals, so it is a survival essential that we are socially aware and kind.

Chapter 10

Filling in the gaps

There are many gaps left open to interpretation. There are gaps in our understanding and things that we cannot answer. Like, how is our memory stored from one life to the next? Memories are stored in our physical brain so how can they be transferred across a time when we have no physical brain?

We can store information electromagnetically; old audio tapes were electromagnetic, even computers store information electromagnetically. So perhaps when we leave the body the form we take is electromagnetic and we carry our memories in some way similar to the way information is stored in a computer. After all, most of our inventions copy nature.

This might even explain some of the fragmentation of memory; an electromagnetic storage system can lose information if there is damage, or over time.

Fragments of memory can be frustrating. When I was in Norway for a conference some years ago I found myself sitting waiting for a while and there was a Norwegian newspaper on a table next to me. I ended up reading an article on the front page about the male contraceptive pill, then realised that it was in Norwegian; I didn't understand any Norwegian, yet I had read and understood the article. But I still had no idea why I could understand what I was reading.

There are gaps in our memories. Even if you can remember past lives nobody can remember every life they ever had. We have been recycled since the beginning of life on this planet, but the best we can do is to recall a few, mainly recent lives and if we are lucky a whole lot of disjointed fragments. So of course there are gaps, bigger gaps the further back in time you look.

There are of course other kinds of gaps in our lives that we try to fill. Terry Pratchett said 'Most people have some means of filling up the gap between perception and reality'. We can all identify with that, everyone has holes in their lives whether made by the loss of a family member, an opportunity missed or just a sense of underachievement. Many people are inclined to try to fill these gaps with things like chocolate, beer or shopping.

However, psychology tells us that when something happens to us that creates a hole in our lives, we instinctively try to fill it, but the time has passed; it is impossible to change something that has already happened. Trying to compensate for it is unfulfilling. What you need to do is see it as it really is, accept it and move forwards.

This is very relevant to past life research. The fact that you hold on to a memory from another life indicates that its absence, or rather your absence from that life now, has created a gap in your current life.

Rather than trying to fill the gaps inappropriately what we usually need is people. Friends and family are the best balancers in life and help us to understand our connectedness with each other. Making that connection with someone else, helping another person to make that connection themselves, has to be better than escapism in an indulgence that in any case fails to help us.

However, it is known that dissatisfaction is the driving force behind innovation. The best inventors and creators are usually socially inept, not team players and not happy with the way things are; which is why they want change. So dissatisfaction or the need to fill the sense of emptiness is useful and can be a motivator for achievement. It has a purpose. This is ironic when companies consciously seek team players and positive people; they are missing out almost completely on creativity and innovation. 'Creativity is discontent translated into arts'- Eric Hoffer.

There are also gaps in our knowledge and understanding. The period between lives is an area we can only explore by subjective means, but that doesn't rule out using science to help us understand.

After each death and being ejected from the body, there is a tunnel of light leading to the place of our existence between lives. Many of us can recall being sucked through a vortex or tunnel, and then the period that followed.

When I remembered the time between lives I felt that I was a ball of energy in a place filled with light and many other energy balls. These energy balls seemed to emit white light, but I had no idea how I sensed it. The light in the distance became fuzzy, like light reflected from headlights in the fog. There were occasional streaks of blue which were not populated by bubble energies.

Energy can take many forms and can convert from one form to another. A physicist told me that if the energy bubbles were 'seeing' in infra red then the light all around could be infra red but might appear as white light and normally visible light might then be seen as blue. If heat and energy are interchangeable then the energy we exist as in between lives could be partially expressed in terms of infra red heat; so the background light could be created by the energy within as heat.

The part of us that is the energy between lives may continue to have some presence there even when we have physical form here; in other words we may have a physical body and a spiritual one at the same time. There are a few reasons for holding this ancient idea. We can remember past lives and between lives. We can remember being when we have no body and no physical contact with the memories within our brain. And we can remember being in different bodies with different brains, yet the same soul or spirit. So the memories cannot be stored only within our brain. Perhaps the memories are stored within our soul energy.

Hypnosis or meditation seem to improve this memory, suggesting it allows access to a deeper part of us. This could be our spiritual self, a self that exists differently to the way our body does in observable space. Simply, we may spill beyond the containment of our body, or we may superimpose ourselves on several dimensions simultaneously.

My physicist friend suggested that low frequency electromagnetic energy could be an information store, but quantum information storage needs atoms. Photon-photon interactions, which is how light interacts with light at the quantized level, may be a way to store information but it is weak at low levels. However, the mass of energy bubbles could maybe boost this. Or our connection to the other realm could be entirely via atoms allowing for low frequency electromagnetic energy.

I realised a while back that I was reading a lot of science magazines, partly to aid my professional knowledge, but there were huge sections that I didn't understand. So I started to make an effort to understand a broader range of science in the hope that it would help me in my search for answers to the conundrums of reincarnation.

There is quite a bit about whether the soul can exist after death, looking at quantum mechanics. For example a rather scholarly paper by the physicist Henry Strapp:

http://www-physics.lbl.gov/~stapp/Compatibility.pdf

However, many of us will already have accepted that the soul does exist; the evidence of people with past life memories or out-of-body experiences is probably sufficient. What interested me was the where and how, rather than if the soul exists. So one area I looked at was string theory.

Does string theory have a place in a book about reincarnation and our sense of connectedness? Actually it might. The mathematics behind string theory is very complex but the theory itself is quite simple to convey and very relevant.

First, string theory is an attempt to explain how the universe works by looking at the smallest particles inside atoms. You may have heard of the search for a unified theory, or a theory of everything. The reason for this search is because we can explain how most things around us work, like electricity, but when it comes to the tiny particles inside atoms the rules go awry. Things have to be explained in a different way.

This is why a few mathematicians managed to come up with string theory (part of multiverse theory) to explain this. In string theory, the atomic particles are described as having tiny vibrating strings where one end is attached to a different, single dimension. In other words everything is connected to another single dimension at subatomic levels. We partially exist somewhere else at the same time as existing here.

The mathematics shows that there would have to be 11 dimensions one of which is time; fewer or more and the numbers don't work. Our universe may have started when several dimensions collided, three of space and one of time. But for the maths to work there would also have to be many universes separated from each other; which is why string theory is part of M theory or the multiverse theory.

So what does that mean and what is the relevance? People like me have always talked about our connectedness, almost like a mantra. Now string theory says we are all connected to another dimension; everything is connected to another dimension and to everything else via this other dimension. So we may be connected to each other and to all things in our universe via another dimension, a single dimension. However, although a single dimension is unlikely to exist on its own there is no reason why this single dimension itself shouldn't also be connected to other dimensions making it another place.

I have often tried to describe our spirit as being permanently connected to another place, so that when we die our energy is sucked back across as though it's on a piece of elastic that has been cut from the no longer functioning body. Once we are no longer confined to our physical body we seem to be pulled into somewhere else. Now the maths describes not only other dimensions in which we partially exist already, but also other universes.

What if we are pulled across to another dimension in which we already partially exist, which may itself be associated with further dimensions or another universe? I'm not sure if this would explain the continuity of the spirit after death, or how memory could survive death, but it might be a starting point in trying to understand. So our memory store could be in both places at once, but continue over there when we lose our physical body here.

Perhaps a simple way to say this would be to think of our universe like a figure of 8 where one loop of the eight is in the here and now that we are aware of, whilst the other loop is linked to another place. In other words reality could be a pair of conjoined universes. Two interconnected realities, but each part could be very different. It wouldn't be separated like the loops of a figure 8 though, as both sections of the pair would be looped over each other as every single atom would have to interconnect between the two.

Another way to look at it would be to envisage Lewis Carroll's 'Through the Looking Glass'. He describes a mirror world connected to ours but very different. The place people remember between lives is indeed very different, with a great deal of energy.

So string theory gives us a connection to one extra single dimension that is partly outside the known universe. But for a single dimension to exist seems illogical, even unlikely. To be connected to a paired system, could be logical. So when enough dimensions collide to make a universe this might require more dimensions than the three of space and one of time (some scientists think two dimensions of time). We might also need the extra dimension that string theory suggests and that in turn might have to be connected to other dimensions creating a double system.

So, science says we may partly exist in another dimension. Near death experiences and past life memory suggests we are pulled through to a paired universe when the body stops working. This means that both science and our observations agree. Although strictly speaking the other side would be linked to the known universe so in some sense part of it. It would not be able to exist alone any more than this side of the universe could exist alone. So rather than thinking of it as a separate universe it would be better to think of it as the hidden part of this universe.

For the science buffs it might even help to explain where dark matter (hidden mass) exists. Also the rules could easily be slightly different there. For example our universe seems to have weak gravity but this could be balanced by stronger gravity on the unseen side.

The other half of a paired universe could balance this half and might explain the anomalies of particle physics, but also how and why reincarnation works, as well as our connectedness with each other via the other half. We might need to return to a physical form this side just to balance a paired system. It might also explain how we are connected to one another at a fundamental level, allowing for telepathy and other anomalous phenomena.

If our energy crosses between two parts of the same universe, the one we see here and the one where we exist between lives, it would have to be this way for all life. One reason for returning is often believed to be about evolving in all ways. Now that we and other higher animals have self awareness, the aim for improvement might be more subtle, related to our connectedness and responsibility to all life.

With reincarnation, trying to explore the science and mechanism is difficult. But wherever there is a gap in our understanding we should endeavour to find out as much as we can. Even if string theory isn't the answer an overlying but very different place as part of a double universe is still the best way to understand where we go between lives, which has to be an actual place.

At the moment it might not be possible to evidence the science involved, but we still have personal experiences. This is why it is important to study and try to verify the past life case histories, experience and observations.

It is human nature to try to make sense of it all but we can only go so far. In any endeavour there is a point beyond which all we get are more questions. It certainly shouldn't stop us looking, thinking and adapting our ideas as more information becomes available.

There is something else to think about, another gap yet to fill; our future. One thing that happens when you have lived a number of years is that you realise time passes quickly. When the time you remember living stretches out over many lives and thousands of years, before the memory becomes dim in the distant past, you know that time passes much too fast. We move into the next decades and centuries faster than you might imagine, and we are coming back to whatever mess we make of the planet.

Overcrowding causes more problems than people might at first realise. Europe and the USA have a below replacement birth rate and for some countries this has been the case for at least 40 years. Most of the population growth in the world is in sub-Saharan Africa, North Africa and the Middle East according to The Telegraph.
http://www.telegraph.co.uk/news/worldnews/11414064/How-Europe-is-slowly-dying-despite-an-increasing-world-population.html).

But it makes no difference where people are born because people have always moved about and always will. Whatever people might think about it, migration is normal. Most of us have ancestors from different parts of the world.

The increasing influx of people to Europe and other developed parts of the world has created a huge rise in population in these areas. Britain, for example, is now only able to produce enough food for 60% of its population and in common with the rest of Europe looks to sub-Saharan Africa to buy in the extra food it needs. This provides an income there, but in the long term may be to the detriment of that part of the world.

Where I live we are seeing a tenfold increase in population and it has spiralled so rapidly that the roads and infrastructure are no longer able to cope. This is a trend happening in many places.

The most common response to overcrowding is mental health problems, though for some it's violence, or escape through drug or alcohol use. The World Heath Organisation cited mental health as a fast growing problem in all developed countries.
(https://www.mentalhealth.org.uk/statistics/mental-health-statistics-uk-and-worldwide)

In the 1950s and 60s many people thought that we would mess the world up with nuclear war. But around 1966 when I was 13, I was more worried about global warming.

It was after my geography teacher showed us photographs of her trip to Norway in 1965 that I realised there was a problem. In some of these photographs large markers could be seen placed in the ground indicating the extent of melting of a glacier, year on year. From this point on I was aware that we had global warming and it seemed completely obvious that we were the cause. But it was many years before anyone was talking about it seriously.

Although Svante Arrhenius, who won the Nobel Prize for Chemistry in 1903, first published his calculations of global warming from human emissions of CO_2 in 1896 it wasn't until around 1977 that scientists began to agree that there was a global warming trend. The World Climate Research Programme was launched in 1979. Mainstream politics only began to discuss greenhouse gases in 1983.

It soon became obvious to me in the 1960s that the warming had started at the beginning of the Industrial Revolution, that it was unnaturally rapid and that we must be the cause, starting with the increased burning of coal for industry. I also knew that warmer air held more moisture (it holds about 5% more moisture for each 1 degree C temperature increase), so had anticipated an increased rainfall, severe storms and flood risks, all of which have happened faster in recent years than even the climate scientists expected. But in 1966 nobody wanted to listen to a teenager with an idea.

Over the past 30 years the global temperature has shown a linear increase of 0.16 degrees C for each decade. In the USA 60% of the land now suffers drought as do parts of India and Eastern Europe. More frequent El Nino conditions are warming the oceans' surface causing record temperatures. The oceans are soaking up some of the heat, but unfortunately it is now known that greenhouse gases we produce are warming the planet by reducing heat loss into space, hence the steady build up of heat, which cannot escape as it normally should.

Forests, especially tropical rain forests, have been absorbing some of the surplus greenhouse gases; which has helped over past decades. But that is slowing as they reach saturation or maximum uptake. We also have to remember that when the earth was much younger and the sun much warmer, only a 6 degree higher temperature meant that the Antarctic was a tropical rain forest and much of the world was uninhabitable.

Research by Jan Esper of Johannes Gutenberg University, Mainz, Germany used tree rings and the chemical air trapped in glacial ice to show that we were in a period of global cooling from at least 2,000 years ago, slowly going towards another ice age, but this was reversed by the Industrial Revolution and all that followed.

In other words it took nearly 2,000 years for the earth to cool a little, and only the last 200 years for us to heat it back up again, and most of that was in the last fifty years.

Bringing the two problems of overpopulation and global warming together it is easy to see that a major solution for both would be a population reduction. Fewer people use fewer resources and produce less CO_2. Even the CO_2 production by cattle would reduce if the human population were much smaller, as their requirements would be proportionately smaller too.

Persistent organic pollutants are reducing the birth rate by rendering some men sterile, which does affect birth rates but not as much as may have been anticipated, yet.

In many places people have already decided that smaller families are better, fairer and easier to support. Having families later also helps as there would be fewer generations alive at the same time. If women have children at age fifteen then seven generations could coexist, but if they had children at age thirty it could be only four generations at best, which is far fewer people. Of course the best way to reduce overpopulation and associated poverty would be to support and empower girls, allow them to stay in school longer and gain a good education and have choice about their own lives.

When parts of the earth become uninhabitable from global warming population control might become a major issue. Tropical areas would be impossible to live in or to grow food in and rising sea levels will shrink the usable land mass everywhere. As people become restricted to ever smaller habitable areas the land left for growing food will become

drastically reduced. With a rising population there will be a point when this becomes a critical problem.
(http://bigthink.com/strange-maps/what-the-world-will-look-like-4degc-warmer)

When most people think about climate change they tend to be psychologically restricted to what might happen in their own country, their own lifetime, or perhaps that of their children. But from my point of view, the people following us are going to be us again. When we think about the future I feel that we must consider it on a different scale, one of centuries and one with us living in it.

We will be coming back to this and cannot guarantee where we will be living. It's probably time to take this thing seriously.

Chapter 11

Carrousel

For most people who recall a past life there isn't enough detail to identify the person. So how do you resolve your feelings so that you can move on? What you can do is identify everything else, like historical context and sometimes location hints. All you need to do is enough to be able to let go of the past and get on with your life.
The amount of research you need to do to find your resolution will vary from person to person but in my case, because I have a tendency to be single-minded and somewhat obsessive, that usually means absolutely everything possible. I find that if I've done everything I can then it's easier to let it go.
Although most past lives are remembered in childhood sometimes events in your life can trigger memories as an adult, or expand the detail of what you recall. There are a number of lives that I remember in fragments that I only pieced together later. The life as Charles was a bit like that, but before I researched that life another one was on my mind. It was of a deaf boy in the 1600s.
You never know when the memory of a past life will begin to intrude into the present, or why. But I am fairly sure that this one came back strongly when it did because I had stopped searching altogether and should have been trying to trace Charles Savage's relatives. I think it was there to prompt me to get on with it.
Running up to the Christmas holiday period of 2009, and for a number of weeks into the new year, the roads were made extremely difficult to negotiate due to repeated heavy snow storms. Because I live and work in a relatively rural area, the roads were at times quite impassable and even when usable, required a great deal of concentration, slow speeds and care. Even with these precautions I managed to slide a few times trying to get around the villages and on one occasion slid

backwards down a hill ending up in snow drifts at the roadside dangerously close to the village pond. So when I felt agitated, tired and slightly detached I assumed it was because of the weather and worry about the problems it caused.

Then one Saturday in January I found myself searching the Internet for a British sign language site. I had wanted to learn sign language since childhood but never questioned why. Indeed I had pestered a girl at junior school to teach me how to sign the letters of the alphabet. She had learnt at Brownies and luckily was patient with me until I got it. She didn't seem to mind; she had been trying to show a group of girls and none of them had been interested, but I was very interested. I then taught my older brother and we used this via a series of mirrors to communicate when we were supposed to be asleep, which must have helped to reinforce the learning.

Over the years I had tried a number of times to find somewhere to learn sign language properly, but without success. The closest I got was a course at a local adult learning centre in the 1980s, but when I applied to book and pay for the course I was told it was only for people who were deaf or becoming deaf and was turned away. I hadn't thought about it for years.

But now I had found sign language on the Internet and was soon learning how to sign. Within days I was able to try out the few signs I had learnt on a deaf lady I worked with on occasion. We had already communicated using the finger spelling I learnt as a child but it was slow. For forty years she had been writing things down because people didn't understand her when she spoke so was delighted that I was trying to learn.

Soon I put myself under a great deal of pressure to learn as much sign language as I could in as little time as possible; I was obsessed. Within three weeks I had more than a hundred words and was pushing to learn a few more every day. Within a month I had mostly grasped the thousand words on a CD. Then found several text books to work from and level 1 and 2 BSL course material.

That was when the memories began to become more prominent. I was washing and remembered times when I had to wash in cold water; then was instantly taken back four hundred years to the 1600s. I was standing in a large barn where cut timber was being stored and where my father worked. I could see what was going on but was not fully involved; I felt isolated. Things were going on around me but nothing was explained, so I couldn't completely understand. This was because I was a deaf boy and had to figure things out for myself.

The memory was one I had visited previously a number of times over the years and had mentioned briefly in my previous books. Despite being deaf in that past life and needing to be able to communicate, I was quite certain there was no proper sign language for me then, just a few hand signals. On the day I remember most and always seem to focus on, I was a boy in my early teens. I always felt that this was around the 1630s.

The barn was wide open at one end and men would come in several at a time carrying fairly long pieces of timber on their shoulders which were then set down onto slim supports. The wood was hefty and smelled fresh and new, yet slightly acrid. Subsequent layers of timbers created almost a lattice effect with the thin supports crosswise and the heavy pieces of wood lengthways down the barn. There were narrow areas where air might pass between the huge timbers. This continued until there was a raft of carefully stacked wood. Over a period of time the stack grew and one side of the barn was mostly filled.

The floor of the barn was just dry dirt which had a slight yellowy tinge of a clay soil and only a light smell suggesting that it had been very dry for quite a while. On top of this were scraps of dry grass, either the remains of grass that had been growing when the barn was built or of hay that had been stored there previously.

There was a mild curve to the uprights where I stood near the entrance. Looking closely I could see that they flared in slightly as they went up and moved inwards towards the apex. The general effect was to soften the edges of the opening to the barn giving a slightly rounded shape to the triangular opening. The two uprights were then topped with a pitch roof. I made a note of this hoping to search barn construction to find out more.

Internally there was an exposed timber frame, consisting of uprights and open roof trusses. Although the building seemed large to me it was only single storey and maybe 15- 18 feet or so wide and its length was perhaps 20 feet, maybe a bit more. The timber stretched almost the entire length of the barn. The walls had a rough texture to them so may have been wattle and daub.

Outside there was a yard big enough for two carts with woodland beyond a field to the left. A rough track passed by close to the side of the new barn and continued a little way beyond the farm.

In front of me were low buildings suitable for animals; pigs judging from the smell. To my right were a few more buildings and the house, which was quite small, single-storied and only had two rooms. The barn was the newest and largest building. Although not huge it dwarfed the house and outbuildings, which were quite modest and in some need of repair.

This is, I think, fairly typical of a past life memory, with quite a bit of detail but only of a few isolated events. As an adult you can expect the memory at first to be like a rough outline, some small event, or a few subtle feelings. It can remain like this if left alone, but thinking about it more of the time, draws you closer in. If you concentrate on it, eventually even tiny minutiae might come into sharp focus. It is the same with any memory; just because this related to a past life there was no difference. If you concentrate on a memory then slowly more comes back. This is worth trying for practice. You need the detail to trace anything about the life.

I could remember a brown spaniel with crinkly soft hair. I had no proper bed but slept on straw and a bundle of rags and the dog slept by me. The room was about ten feet square with a fire on the outside wall which abutted the animal sheds; it was squalid and the floor was just dry dirt. One day I suddenly remembered that the dog died when I, the boy, was about ten years old and I cried at the loss of my closest friend. There were no siblings or mother but it wasn't unusual for a woman to die in childbirth.

This memory was filled with smells so vivid that they almost had another dimension to them. Research shows that people who are blind utilise the area usually used for sight, in order to learn Braille. So it is possible that without hearing or language, some of the brain would be available for other uses, such as a more complex appreciation of smell. Amusingly in my current life my sense of smell is good; Several times I have managed to sniff out and find a chip shop from many streets away when others with me had no inkling that it was there.

Because smells are very closely linked to memory, specific smells are capable of triggering a complex array of remembered feelings and events. I recalled the chickens and was aware of their warm mellow tang and the earth, dry and savoury, or damp and rich after the rain. In a musty sacking apron I had sweet smelling grain, which was cast on the ground for the chickens which fussed around me pecking in the dirt.

The aroma of the pigs was richer and more complex. Their heavy sweet sweat reminded me of bacon cooking. And there was the strong odour of the valuable manure mixed with straw, which I dug out of the sty and carried to a heap behind the outbuildings. I felt that there were not many pigs and we may not have a pig all of the time.

On that day when the wood was being carried into my father's barn I was aware that there was another dog; my father's large black working dog that was tied up in the yard.

The best clue to start with was the barn, which was a similar size to a pre-war small hay barn. It was airy, perhaps to allow air to flow around the wood, and the large entrance may have been for easy access for the timber and for carts. I could remember the feel of the curved and substantial front supports used at the opening.

The mild musty acrid smell of the wood being stored in the barn was completely recognisable. In my current life I have worked with wood as a hobby from childhood onwards. A few years ago I made a garden bench from oak; the strong smell of oak is quite distinctive, so I knew that the barn was made from oak and that the wood being stored was also oak.

Once you think you have a clear picture of the memory the next step is to try to research what you have. My feeling was that this was Britain but I needed to find something to back this up. I found that in Britain oak was the commonest tree and was used extensively in ship building from the time of the Spanish Armada to Nelson's day and has always been used for making furniture. The Spanish naval expedition against England was in 1588 and Nelson died in 1805. So if this was in England then the oak I saw could easily have been used for ship building in the 1600s.

I wondered why the timbers were stacked under cover. In modern times I had seen cut timber stacked outside to weather. The local woodland is managed and forested and I often walk there. Also I had seen wood stacked for sale in timber yards, but it was not usually laid with gaps. I had not in my present life seen wood stacked the way I remember in the 1600s barn.

So I turned to a very useful source of information. My husband's professional knowledge of building materials and methods is extensive, so I thought he would be able to help. He was able to tell me that oak was laid on narrow batons and with gaps between to allow air to circulate while the wood was seasoned. This was usually done under cover if the wood had been cut and planed. The wood I remember had indeed been cut and planed and had been stacked on batons.

I asked Steve what the wood would be used for if it was quite long and had a 'this size' square profile, as I held up my hands to show the size. We measured the square gap between my hands and found it to be almost exactly six inches. Steve then told me that the standard sizes for oak used for general building construction was 6 x 6 inches or 8 x 8 inches square.

This told me that the wood might be being seasoned for general building use rather than ship building. I asked Steve if the rest of Europe would have used a different standard but he said it would have been similar, because you are limited by the girth of tree that can be cut with the type of saw used at the time, and the girth dictated the size of the cut timber. Huge trees were much too hard to cut down and standardised sizes were needed so that when the timber was used for building the joints could match up and work properly. So it could have been anywhere in Europe.

I needed to find out more about the barn structure. The style of the barn might pinpoint the location if I was lucky. Several hours on the Internet took me slightly further, although most of the barns I found were very much larger stone or brick-built tithe barns. These were used to store the Church taxes as one tenth of the local produce. Some of them were huge with an intricate support structure inside, a bit like my barn but very much larger and with many more supports.

The American sites had more about the history of barns than British sites. They referred to an English barn dating from about 1770, which was too squared to be my barn and a bit large. They did have large paired doors that opened up at one end to allow access for a fully laden cart. The framework was generally covered with boards.

Most of the barns from around the time-frame were built in oak. I found out that the reason oak had to be seasoned so carefully was that the pegged joints would fail if green wood was used and it dried out after construction and could warp. By the end of the 17th century there was pressure on domestic oak in England.

I found a traditional oak building company and looking at the details tried to find out if the construction methods made the uprights seem to curve as they met roof trusses, but I couldn't see that curve anywhere. So I talked to Steve again, this time about the curved uprights which I described to him. Steve suggested that I try looking at cruck barns, which were built with curved timbers.

Further research led me to discover that cruck barns probably evolved in Anglo Saxon times and the earliest excavation of one was in Buckinghamshire; this dated to the 4th century. They came into their own in the Middle Ages when they were seen as a status symbol of a farmer's wealth. This might explain why my father in that life had a big new barn but only a modest farm house; it was a bit like buying a flash new Range Rover nowadays; he was showing off.

Cruck barns were built with 'A' frames of oak at each end, sometimes split long ways from the same tree to get the curve of the timbers to match up. The beams were joined at the apex by a tie beam. The advantage of the design was that the framework could be light as the roof load was carried directly to the ground. This was the only kind of barn construction that matched the barn of my memories.

By the 18th century cruck frame barns went out of fashion as box framing became more successful and used less wood. So my barn in the 17th century fits very well as a traditional cruck-framed barn, at the very time when they were at their height in England.

This was the strongest detail of the memory that seemed to locate the life as being in England; the archetypal cruck barn. The structure of the barn also helped to confirm that the time period was likely to be right.

On a journey to visit my mother I discussed the floor of the farm house with Steve. I told him that all I could see was dirt and straw. He said that was all I would see, the floor would have been compacted earth, or if they had it, some local material of firmer structure, like a mix of sand or rough gravel compressed into the surface. This would then be covered with straw which could be changed from time to time to clean it out. A proper floor would have been too expensive. I told him that I couldn't see any furniture and I slept on straw in the floor. Steve's reply was that even quite wealthy houses from the period only had a few items of furniture, so he wasn't surprised. When we got to my mother's home -she is a retired science teacher and an active amateur historian- she told me exactly the same thing.

When I was standing near the front of the barn, the sun shone directly on the front all day, but the outbuildings were in the shade for most of the day. I felt that the sun moved across from the left, from slightly behind the outbuildings, then towards the right where it came across enough to light the front of the house slightly. That would make the barn facing roughly south-east. Slowly the picture was becoming clearer; details were beginning to add up and make sense.

Over the next couple of weeks I thought about more details and realised that I recalled a short trip into the village, roughly to the north-west, on a cart with my father. We must have been on slightly higher ground briefly because from the cart, as we passed the trees and approached the village, I could see the sea to my right. This would probably put the farm close to the east coast. The coast line itself would be running almost north with about a five degree western tilt.

So what I needed to look for was an area of coastline in the east of England where the land was fairly flat. The angle of the coast that I remembered would also be helpful. This was enough to draw a sketch map. I had the direction of east, because I could remember the sun moving across in front of the barn through the day. And I knew that the sea was to the east, because I could see it on the cart journey. This detail gave me the opportunity of producing an accurate portrayal of the area. Now I had some chance of finding a location.

Looking for the correct angle of the coast line it seemed to be limited to a couple of places on the north coast of Suffolk, one was around Lowestoft.

I checked in a book of county maps by the early Victorian map maker Thomas Moule, first published in 1830, but there were no relevant maps. Even at that time most of the modern coastal towns were little more than small villages. By then some had a station, as the railway lines steadily expanded to take people to the coast. This meant that the nearby village I recalled could now be a busy town, swallowing up the site of the farm and fields altogether.

Although towns had changed a great deal, most of the small villages marked on a modern map also existed in the 1830s. As to roads, there was, of course, no way of knowing which tracks from the Middle Ages had been adopted as modern roads and surfaced. However, it was likely that the dead end farm track I remembered would never have become a proper road and may not even be a farm any more.

Something else that affected map changes, especially in the countryside, was the Black Death. It first reached England in

1348, but the last outbreak was in 1665. In this final attack it wiped out whole villages and one tenth of London's population. As people deserted villages and farms that were affected, some places completely disappeared from maps. A few deserted mediaeval villages can still be found marked on modern maps but there is nothing to see at ground level; they are only revealed by archaeology. This was worryingly close to the period I was looking at; the boy could have been around fifty in 1665.

There were a couple of possible sites but owing to the amount of change I eventually realised that it wasn't going to be possible to get a more accurate location.

Now it was my job to make sense of it all. My feeling was that many questions remained unanswered. However, I realised that sign language was still important so decided to look further at that.

The signed BBC programme 'See Hear' had a new item giving a history of sign language. Briefly, the first recorded use of sign language was in 1576. The parish archives for Leicester record a marriage between Ursula Russell and a local deaf man Thomas Tilsve. His signs, which were agreed upon beforehand, were acknowledged by the church and the law as his acceptance of the vows of marriage. Few signs were described but he did mime the tolling of a bell to recognise his vows which is similar to the modern BSL sign for church.

So my memory of having no proper sign language some few decades later would be likely if the first few signs were only just beginning to be used some decades earlier.

For me, this life from long ago probably insinuated itself into my consciousness because it represented unfinished business and was a gateway to facing up to my memory as Charles in Gateshead. We remember past lives for many reasons. It is not always necessary to research them, sometimes all we need to do is acknowledge feelings that we need to address.

However, even with relatively little information it is possible to check enough historical detail to find some degree of confirmation. The whole goal of the exercise is to let go and move on with your life. There have been enough high profile cases to provide good evidence for reincarnation, so that is no longer a huge necessity. What matters to the person experiencing past life memories is closure; closure is always possible even without finding out exactly who you were.

Conclusion

We may not all be able to remember our previous lives, we are probably not meant to, but we should still be able to benefit from the experiences learnt in those lives anyway. We are who we are partly because of our past experiences, whether they occurred recently or in another life long ago and whether we can remember them or not. Actually remembering the lives themselves is less important than how we learn from our past; we are all connected in life's journey and rely on each other's support.

My search for past life families is probably very much over. Finding John Savage and resolving my most recent past life memory as his brother Charles, felt different. I knew that it was probably the last life left with enough detail to be able to research; it was finally time to let go of a lifetime obsession.

But of course the memories themselves will never end or completely fade. More detail will no doubt rise to the surface from time to time and I will think back over the lives I have always remembered, but now with fondness; the worry is no longer relevant.

I have found my families; the people I needed to find, and resolved so many past lives. Through a lifetime of researching past life memories, I have been lucky to be able to look back knowing that what I remember is what actually happened. I have also had the good fortune to share the journey with the many people who have kindly given their time to aid the research effort, and to my great joy, with those who could remember and confirm the lives of the people I recall.

But these searches that I have shared with you, with all of their ups and downs, have not just been about me or even entirely for me. The message I have always tried to share is that this is about all of us. We all come back, we are all connected and we will all share the future together.

My search for the past has set me free at last. I no longer feel driven to look back to resolve past issues. I can now do what I have always said we are supposed to do with our lives, live it, share it with others, enjoy it and move forwards.

Links

Jenny Cockell- reincarnation and the "children of yesterday"
https://www.youtube.com/watch?v=GLkgr7mbP5o

Printed in Great Britain
by Amazon